KALEIDOSCOPE

NORTH CHESHIRE

Edited by Simon Harwin

CW01430334

First published in Great Britain in 1999 by
POETRY NOW YOUNG WRITERS
Remus House, Coltsfoot Drive,
Woodston,
Peterborough, PE2 9JX
Telephone (01733) 890066

All Rights Reserved

Copyright Contributors 1998

HB ISBN 0 75430 377 2
SB ISBN 0 75430 378 0

FOREWORD

This year, the Poetry Now Young Writers' Kaleidoscope competition proudly presents the best poetic contributions from over 32,000 up-and-coming writers nationwide.

Successful in continuing our aim of promoting writing and creativity in children, each regional anthology displays the inventive and original writing talents of 11-18 year old poets. Imaginative, thoughtful, often humorous, *Kaleidoscope North Cheshire* provides a captivating insight into the issues and opinions important to today's young generation.

The task of editing inevitably proved challenging, but was nevertheless enjoyable thanks to the quality of entries received. The thought, effort and hard work put into each poem impressed and inspired us all. We hope you are as pleased as we are with the final result and that you continue to enjoy *Kaleidoscope North Cheshire* for years to come.

CONTENTS

Jennifer Ann Simister	68
Eve Barry	68
Frances Morgan	69
Nicola Furniss	70
Siobhan Lillie	71
Christina Murphy	72
Clare Rushton	73
Felicity Woof	74
Colette McGrory	74
Lauren Morell	75
Emma Stuart	76
Caroline Dunne	76
Helen Phillips	77
Victoria Stott	77
Catherine Hamilton	78
Jemma Cosgrove	79
Katie Brown	80
Philippa Brown	80
Michelle Mullen	81
Bernadette Thompson	82
Louise Daley	83
Christine Armstrong	83
Rachel Taylor	84
Joanne Grant	84
Helen Sweeney	85
Siobhan O'Grady	86
Andrea Klikucs	86
Victoria Briffa	87
Aimée Beech	88
Vanessa Rigby	88
Rebecca Wellock	89
Camilla Woof	90
Charlene Maher	91
Karen Finney	92
Katie Serridge	92
Julia Price	93
Kate Wickstone	94
Victoria Sumner	94

Melissa Kidd	95
Emily Towey	96
Lucy Abdulla	96
Katie Lewis	97
Suzanne Murray	98
Robyn Massey	98
Joanne Keys	99
Angela Hardman	100
Helen Tansley	101
Sophie Jackson	101
Anna Clarke	102
Claire Toland	102
Rachael Murdoch	103
Sarah Peat	103
Jessica Robinson	104
Rachel Clarke	104
Jemma Egan	105
Fiona McGuire	106
Louise Buxton	107
Katie Davies	107
Katie Mellett	108
Sarah Chester	108
Laura Callan	109
Helen Ward	110
Kate Gaughan	110
Hayley Smith	111
Sarah Hepple	112
Jenny Bazill	113
Emma Divinney	114
Rebecca Swarbrick	115
Charlotte Burton	116
Beth Westwood	117
Vicky Brown	118
Laura McNally	118
Eleanor Smith	119
Anne Marie Collins	120
Mariann Martinez	120
Michelle Dooley	121

The Poems

STAR SIGNS

From Aries to Pisces, 12 different signs,
Everyone is something, no one is excluded.

Some people scoff at the whole idea,
Others follow it religiously.
But why pay attention to a bunch of burning balls of gas?
Why let them predict and direct our future?
The entire concept is insanity itself, isn't it?

I know people who are typical of their 'sign',
And others who are the opposite.
But then again, those who believe are typical,
Those who don't are not.

Some may say that they were a week early and were meant to be a . . .
Ah, so that explains it, or are they just superstitious fools too?

Ancient civilisations swore by the signs of the Zodiac,
And they led good lives,
But then, they are just ancient figments of the past.
So should we, could we, would be believe,
That it was invented by intuition alone?
By people who just wanted to explain why things are the way they are?

Well, I for one say each to their own.
For all I have just written just proves I am a typical Pisces!

Laura M Corcoran (13)
Loreto Grammar School

WHAT WOULD EARTH BE LIKE WITHOUT LIGHT?

What would Earth be like without light?
A big, black hole without life.
No people, no sound, no whispering voices in the street.
Nothing.

What would Earth be like without life?
An empty sphere without feelings.
No joy, no happiness, no love and no belief.
Nothing.

What would Earth be like without feelings?
A dark cavity filled with crime.
No responsibility, no caring, no respect for others.
Nothing.

What would Earth be like without life?
Nothing.

Nicola Watterson (13)
Loreto Grammar School

WRITING POETRY

I'm rubbish at writing poems,
I suppose I'm just uninspired,
If only they could write themselves,
Maybe it's that my brain's expired.

Nobody really knows the rules of poetry,
Rhyming or not?
You could write one about anything,
Even gnomes living in a pot.

I'm rubbish at writing poems,
There's not one idea in my head,
I need an idea pretty quickly,
Or 'Miss' will make sure I end up dead.

Hey look what I've just written,
I'm great at writing poems,
My next masterpiece will be on a fluffy kitten,
'Miss' will be impressed!

Julaine Speight (13)
Loreto Grammar School

THE MIDNIGHT CAT

'Click' the last light was flicked off.
The house was silent apart from
The humming of the refrigerator,
From under the kitchen table,
Two large yellow eyes blinked.
A furry form uncoiled itself,
Arched its back
And spread out its claws.
A body and a long slender tail,
Emerged from the darkness.
Tail in the air it stole fluidly
Across the cold, stony floor.
Its mackerel striped fur
Glinted in a stray shaft of moonlight.
Ears straining for sound,
Whiskers scanning for movement.
A bold leap through the cat flap
And out into the exciting darkness beyond.

Helen Toalster (12)
Loreto Grammar School

MY DREAMS

A dream is a wish
Your soul makes,
When you're fast asleep.
You cannot always
Remember it,
But it's something you want to keep.

Sometimes I dream
Of the future,
And how it might
Turn out to be.
I dream of my life
As a singer
And that's how
I want it to be.

I'd sing in front
Of thousands,
On stages all over the world.
People would say
'She's wonderful'
The best we've ever heard.

I hope this dream comes true
I really want it to,
If it does won't I be glad,
If it doesn't I'll be sad.
But there is one thing I know
Dreams can come true!

Rita O'Connor (13)
Loreto Grammar School

ALONE

Here I sit all alone,
Among a room full of people
Bored and on my own.
What am I waiting for?

In he walked,
My dream boy.
My imagination racing,
My heart pounding,
But wait, I'm all alone.

There he was, the boy of my dreams,
But look.
He's coming towards me, it must be me
Because I'm all alone in a corner.

Here he is,
He is talking to me. His name is James.
Do I want to dance?
Yes.
So we did.

Wait we've stopped.
Now I wake up.
In my empty room,
All alone!

Susannah Branney (13)
Loreto Grammar School

FRIENDS

Friends you love them,
You hate them,
But you can be sure a true friend
Is always there.
Through good times and bad,
Through sickness and in health,
A friend is always there to
Pull you through.

You might have a jolly friend,
You might have a moody friend,
But a friend is a friend,
Someone special to you.

You might have one best friend,
Then again you might not,
You may have lots of friends,
All that matters is that you have a friend,
Some friends are for life.

Leanne Oxley (13)
Loreto Grammar School

IS IT A DREAM OR NOT?

As I walked through a dark, scary field,
I could see shadows of the trees,
The trees looked like real people,
I realised they were real.

I could feel the grass on my legs,
And to my horror they were snakes,
They were slimy and long,
Trying to trip me over.

I could see the trees moving,
They were following me,
They were trying to hurt me,
I started to cry, I kept running faster and faster.

The trees now were monsters and grabbed me,
They started shaking me, shouting 'Helen, Helen!'
I came to a sudden halt in this world,
I awoke and came back to reality,
Mum said, 'It was only a dream dear!'

Helen Shaw (13)
Loreto Grammar School

A CAT

He patrolled the streets in the darkest of nights,
Only lit by the dimmest of lights.
His eyes shone green and yellow,
Can you hear his joyful bellow?

His dark silky fur vanished into the swirling mist,
If he came across an intruder he hissed,
And fluffed his tail high and wide,
Then all the other cats ran in to hide.

As morning began to dawn,
Yet another new day was born.
So the cat ran back to his house,
If he was lucky, he'd catch a mouse.

He'd curl up on his bed,
As thoughts ran through his head.
One owner came down, not making a sound,
The sleeping cat he found.

Emily Sleight (12)
Loreto Grammar School

MY SISTER

My sister, urgh, I hate the word.
You're related. Don't remind me.
You look awfully alike. Please don't go on.
You get on so well. No I don't want
To hear anymore.

You sit next to her on the bus.
Because I have to.
You talk to her when you see her.
I'm only being polite.
You don't fight. Oh, but we do!

Do you like her? Erm sometimes.
Does she annoy you? Mmm maybe.
Do you get on with her? Possibly.
Is she nice to you? Might be.
Is she fun? Yeah.
So what's your problem? Erm nothing.
So shut up then!

Katherine Kerrigan (13)
Loreto Grammar School

THE PANTHER

In the dark of the night,
its yellow eyes grew bright,
and its claws ready to kill,
with its slender tail,
it couldn't fail,
it had to earn its fill.

The strange sensation,
of concentration,
was ripping through its heart.
The creature screeched,
and dug its teeth,
into its prey like a dart.

Jenny Whiteley (12)
Loreto Grammar School

ALL ON MY OWN

The wind howls,
The shutters rattle,
The doorbell rings,
And the mice scuttle.

I hate it on my own.

The floorboards creak,
The trees rustle,
The door slams,
And the windows shake.

I hate it on my own.

The TV flashes,
The curtains blow,
The phone rings,
But I'm not home.

I hate it on my own.

A car pulls up,
The gravel crunches,
I'm so glad it's you,
I hate it on my own.

Rebecca Cartledge (13)
Loreto Grammar School

THE FEROCIOUS LION

As I was looking for my cat in the park,
I came across a very brightly coloured lark,
He warned me that there was a ferocious lion about,
And that he wandered upon the mount.

As I wandered on, all became dark,
And all I could think of were the wise words given to me from the lark,
The trees were bare and the leaves around my feet were red,
How I wish I was in my cosy bed.

As I walked on, it became even darker,
And the path suddenly stopped,
'Which way should I go?' I had no idea,
I chose a path and wandered on.

Soon I came across a pair of green flashing eyes,
I stood stiff and didn't dare breathe,
The thing moved closer and things became clearer,
It had two fluffy ears, whiskers and a very long tail.

It stepped forward into the light between the trees,
And then it let out a . . .
'Miaow'
It was only my cat Tootsie.

Lauren Kelly (12)
Loreto Grammar School

THE BRAVE TIGER

The tiger is hiding deep in the forest,
Maybe he'll be found.
Nothing will scare him, no one will harm him,
Not even the smallest sound.
He's his own man, fierce and frightening,
Swaying side to side,
His deep inner feelings won't stop the meaning,
From the hunters he's trying to hide.
Sometimes he'll kill to catch his prey
And carry on walking day after day.
He'll stump and squash and carry on fighting,
Then click goes the camera, he's now in the sighting.
People will follow, he'll be dead by tomorrow,
He's being hunted down,
The King of the Jungle has lots his crown.

There is another one gone!

Sophia Vitti (12)
Loreto Grammar School

LUCY

She's curled upon the hearth rug
And yawning in deep content
Accepting all the gifts that providence has sent
Louder she purrs and louder in one joyful hymn of praise
For exciting night adventures and quiet peaceful days.

Georgina Neale (13)
Loreto Grammar School

CHEETAH

The cheetah is a cactus as she lies cunning and still,
There's hunger in her eyes as she prepares to kill!
Her mystic glare is that of a beast,
She analyses her surroundings, for an early evening feast!
Her craving desire is growing stronger,
Her cubs are whining, they cannot wait any longer.
As the sun falls through the trees,
Her prey comes into view, through the sour chilling breeze,
She saunters low through the long green grass,
Her hunger is about to be fulfilled at long last.
Suddenly in the distance a deep scowl is heard,
Bon appetite - dinner is served!

Zara Rizvi (12)
Loreto Grammar School

THE WILD HORSE!

She gallops swiftly through the air,
Without one single care.
Her hairy white mane sweats with joy,
As she wanders across the sandy beach.

Her swirled horn shines, crystal-like in the roasting sun,
And her golden tail swifts slowly side to side
As she glides through the air.
As she picks up her speed her hooves beat faster and faster
Against the gritty sand.

All creatures admire her freedom and long to be her,
But she is one of a kind, she is a unicorn.

Rebecca Creamer (13)
Loreto Grammar School

A Day In The Life Of Tily!

My hamster is tiny, she's brown and white,
She scurries around in the dark of night,
Stopping now and then to have a wash,
Making herself look very posh.
She runs on her wheel and up some stairs,
Having such fun, she just doesn't care.
She has a nibble at some food,
And sometimes gets in a tired mood.
Her name is Tily,
She's sometimes quite silly,
When she plays with her friend Little Billy.
She curls herself into a ball,
Until the break of dawn the next day,
When she comes out again for lots more play.

Sarah Ginder (12)
Loreto Grammar School

A Dog

Vicious prowler
A cuddly companion
A reliable rex
A fast fidgeter
A moaning mongrel
A whining woofer
A mad barker
A trainable tinker
A nosy sniffer
A silly sensor
A playful puppy
A loving licker.

Johanna Gardener (11)
Loreto Grammar School

MAKING NEW FRIENDS

Making new friends is a hard thing to do
Finding a person who likes you.
It takes a long time,
But it is worthwhile
You'll be friends for a long time.

If it doesn't work out
You can find another person,
Who maybe has something in common.
You don't have to be a genius to find a friend.

You can ring every night
To have a good natter.
So go ahead, make a new friend or two.

Elaine Hayes (13)
Loreto Grammar School

A DOG

A furry face
A wet nose
A soft paw
A face licker
A toe biter
A tail wagger
A cuddly creature
A naughty barker
A fierce growler
A friend for life.

Rachael Kovach (11)
Loreto Grammar School

DOLLY AND THE DOLPHIN!

It swims around the swimming pool,
Jumping in and out.
A blue-grey blur,
As fast as lightning it swims around.
That's right, a dolphin!

Dolly jumped in and screamed,
Screamed with glee and delight.
We stood there for ages, ages and ages,
Waiting for Dolly to come out -
She wouldn't.

The dolphin jumped and swam,
Round, up, down, left and right.
It seemed he'd never sleep.
Dolly screamed, Dolly shouted,
Never ever wanting to come out.

Clare Sullivan (13)
Loreto Grammar School

MYSTERY

It is a gurgling giggler,
a loud screamer, a horrible howler,
a mischievous meddler,
and is nosy.
It is a tiny bundle of trouble,
a babbler, a dreadful dribbler,
a sound sleeper,
and a gorgeous grinner.

Victoria Harris (11)
Loreto Grammar School

THE MONKEYS

Out in the forest, within the trees
The monkeys swing under the leaves
From branch to branch and
Tree to tree
They're too busy to see me.

Their arms have a rhythm
That makes them move through the air
There is no danger there
As they jump and they turn
Without a care.

They play their game
And shout out loud
But I'm not playing
I'm staying on the ground.

Jade Gavin (12)
Loreto Grammar School

RAIN

The plant waterer
The crop grower
The pitter-patter on my window sill
The boredom causer
The wet play maker
The gutter filler
The cry for umbrellas
The creator of puddles
The people splasher
The enemy of sun.

Michelle Barrett (12)
Loreto Grammar School

MY YOUNG LOVE

My young love is dead
Gone forever
Never to return
How will I cope?
How will I manage?
He was my fire that burnt within.

My young love is dead
He's disappeared
Left me all alone
How will I cope with the burden of his baby?
How will I manage when it's born?

My young love is dead
Has he just left me?
Or will we meet again some day?
I need him
I love him
He cannot abandon me
He promised to provide for me
How will I survive?

My young love still lives
He has not left me
He will wait for me till the end of time.

Elaine Gough (13)
Loreto Grammar School

HOLIDAYS

Who said holidays were meant to be fun?
The amount of fun ones I've had is none!
Well really that's not all true,
There was that one when I just had the flu.

The holidays aren't always that bad,
It's just things like sand and sunburn that make me mad,
I mean sand, it goes everywhere,
Up your nose, in your hair,
In your sandwiches, between your toes,
Behind your ears, in your clothes,
Why can't sand have larger grains?
The small ones are such a pain!
And sunburn makes me want to scream,
How can God be so mean?
To make us fry like bacon and eggs,
And it makes our skin go scaly like frogs' legs.

Aeroplanes make your eyes pop,
But I do like the duty-free shop,
The flight attendants are always nice,
On my last trip I got a free glass of champagne, twice!

I really hate holidays, I really do,
I think I'd be better sticking to Blackpool,
Don't you?

Hollie Yates (13)
Loreto Grammar School

THESE I HAVE LOVED

These I have loved:
The sweet smell of tarmac, as it has just been put down;
The clouds passing by the moon, on a very cloudy night;
Blue ribbons that little girls wear, on their way to school;
The way grey school trousers suddenly turn black,
as soon as they have just finished a good game of football;
Sleep;
All the wonderful different colours of the rainbow;
Television;
The way all the food in the cupboard disappears within a few days;
Music;
The sound of horseshoes clopping against the ground,
as it trots past you;
And last of all, the way rabbits soon find their burrows when
someone comes near.

Kerri Johnson (13)
Loreto Grammar School

HOUSE

Red brick
Brown wood
Trees and plants
Shining glass
Familiar smells
Familiar people
Warm and cosy
Welcoming.

Joanne Connor (12)
Loreto Grammar School

CATS

Cats have unusual tongues,
when you feel them they're dry and rough.
Cats sit curled up in a ball
like a ball of cotton wool.
They purr contentedly like a distant volcano
getting ready to erupt.
Their eyes have an ebony almond inside them,
overloaded with unknown emotions.
Their whiskers are stiff
like the strings of a violin bow.
Cats walk with pride and elegance,
they lift up their paws properly
and place them down carefully.
Cats are amazing
almost human sometimes.

Leila Faddoul (13)
Loreto Grammar School

HAIKU

In the dull churchyard
The wind blew through the trees
A strange air hung.

Her eyes were tearful
The photo clasped in her hands
Her body shaking.

Frances Hughes (12)
Loreto Grammar School

SILENCE!

Silence is precious,
Especially to me,
I hate the noisy traffic,
And the crying baby.

I love to be alone,
Just my book and me,
Lying on my bed,
Or sitting in a tree.

I love the song of birds,
Or the buzzing of the bees,
It's my brother and sister shouting,
That really gets to me.

I love to lie on my bed,
Absorbed into my book,
But if there's noise around me,
Then there isn't any luck.

I can't take in the story,
Or even focus on the words,
When there's noise around me,
It's totally absurd!

That's why silence is precious,
To all those who are like me,
Who don't want noisy atmospheres,
While they're trying to read.

Rebecca Murray (13)
Loreto Grammar School

NIGHT

The night is dark, strange and mystical,
Full of all the unexplainable,
Shadows will creep
As the world will sleep
In the cold, frosty, unearthly night.

The night is secret, silent and still,
Full of things that should not live,
Creatures will screech
As the hidden will reach
For the moonlit, shadowy, scary night.

The night is frozen, black and lethal,
Full of sounds that are not spoken,
Eyes will watch
As bats will cross
Through the shady, deadly, puzzling night.

Elizabeth Locke (11)
Loreto Grammar School

THE CAT

The milk licker,
The cat flap clicker.
The careful creeper,
The little mouse seeker.
The sharp clawed creature,
The baby kitten teacher.
The bright eyed daydreamer,
The dark night road lighter.
The fur coated street walker,
The cunningly quiet bird stalker.

Lizzy Allman (12)
Loreto Grammar School

EMPTY

I'm empty,
All alone in this enormous world,
Oh what to do?

I used to be one of a pair,
I used to be fun and outgoing.
But now you're gone there is nothing left here for me
But memories.
Now you're gone, I'm nothing,
Nothing I am.
Oh why did you leave me on this big scary world alone?

I looked up to heaven and saw your face,
It made me cry,
And reminded me of one thing,
That one thing is,
I'm empty.

Vicki Sadler (13)
Loreto Grammar School

THE SQUIRREL

Silently slipping through the darkness,
Padding quietly through the night black.
Creeping in the forest glade,
Climbing in the trees up high,
Playing in the leaves near the sky.
The sun is rising so she disappears,
Into a black oak hollow.

Lauren O'Toole (12)
Loreto Grammar School

A POEM IS A VERY STRANGE THING

A poem is a very strange thing,
It does not leap about or sing,
Yet when you read aloud in class,
You feel as if you're breathing gas.

A poem is a very strange thing,
It may not heckle, bounce or swing,
But one thing on which it does depend,
Is a good beginning, middle and end.

A poem is a very strange thing,
It does not go ting-a-ling,
Although many of them are written for kings,
Poems are still, very strange things.

Amanda Lukeman (13)
Loreto Grammar School

THE CAT

Her large green eyes peer
From the darkness.
Slowly she approaches.
Her long tail waves in the air
Her ears are pricked.
She pauses and looks round
Selecting her sleeping place.
Sleepily she walks to her chosen spot.
She moves round in small circles
Then curls up tight.
She glances round, shuts her eyes
And sleeps.

Sarah Pennington (13)
Loreto Grammar School

IMAGINE

A world where people walk upright
Where electric lamps light up the night
Where animals are kept as pets
Where days are dry and sometimes wet
Where skies are blue but never green
Where the wind is heard but never seen
Where stars shine in the sky at night
Where a yellow sun gives warmth and light
Where seas are calm but sometimes rough
Where there's lots of food but never enough
Where children play while parents worry
Where everyone is in a hurry
Where the moon is small and far away
Where 24 hours equals one day
Where all life starts with a baby's birth
If you haven't guessed it, this is our Earth.

Kelly Timmins (13)
Loreto Grammar School

A HAMSTER

There once was a very small hamster,
Who was quite a real prankster,
When he was in bed,
We thought he was dead,
And he turned out to be Harry the Gangster.

Sarah Leahy (12)
Loreto Grammar School

MY EVERYTHING

The depth of sparkle in your perfect eyes,
The streak of mischief you possess deep inside,
The sense of perfection in your great stride,
The sudden burst of inspiration I feel when you're by my side.

The way you stand high and proud,
Deep inside me there is a voice that shouts out loud,
The way your thoughtful smile highlights my day,
The way your glistening hair shines in the sun's rays.

The way your sensitive and charming side shines through,
The sense of success I feel when I'm around you,
The way your perfect teeth always gleam,
Forever you will remain in my reoccurring dream.

The way your voice expresses you really care,
Nobody could break the eternal bond we share,
The glimpse of burning passion in your heart,
The instant urge for us never to be apart.

Elizabeth Kenny (13)
Loreto Grammar School

DOLPHINS

On the surface there's little motion,
but it's very different under the ocean.
As the fish fly through the sea,
the dolphins sing playfully.

They zoom around chasing tails,
swimming around the fish and whales.
They meet some fish and say hello,
then wave goodbye and off they go.

They dart around the corals and rocks,
then off they go to visit the docks.
They do some tricks, the people cheer,
and throw enough fish to last a year.

Then off they go homeward bound,
they dash through the water without a sound.

Laura Fallon (13)
Loreto Grammar School

MY GARDEN

My garden is where:
The birds cheep cheerfully,
The frogs are the slimiest,
The foxes cry the loudest,
The bees buzz all day,
The dogs bark loudly,
and the hopping bunnies twitch,
That's my garden.

My garden is where:
The pool is bright and deep,
The blackbird sings the latest tune,
The nestlings chirp and flee,
and the mower mows the neatest,
That's my garden.

My garden is where:
The stars are mellow,
The moon silently watches the world go by,
The trees sway rhythmically in the breeze,
The dew rests upon the lush grass,
and the spiders spin their silver webs,
That's my garden.

Caroline Woolf (13)
Loreto Grammar School

TEN YOUNG SCHOOLGIRLS

Ten young schoolgirls drinking wine
One got drunk
And then there were nine
Nine young schoolgirls staying up late
One never woke up
And then there were eight
Eight young schoolgirls studying about heaven
One went to find it
And then there were seven
Seven young schoolgirls picking up sticks
One went off into the woods
And then there were six
Six young schoolgirls went for a dive
One never returned
And then there were five
Five young schoolgirls using a saw
One chopped herself in half
And then there were four
Four young schoolgirls climbing a tree
One fell out
And then there were three
Three young schoolgirls with toys very new
One lost hers
And then there were two
Two young schoolgirls playing in the sun
One got sunburnt
And then there was one
One sad schoolgirl not having any fun
She went home alone
And then there were none.

Maria Winstanley (13)
Loreto Grammar School

WHALE POEM

W hales, majestic creatures, we only
   glimpse as they rise from the deep,
H iding under the ocean they play out
   their rich social lives,
A lways they are listening to the sounds
   of the deep and the fish they seek,
L oudly they signal their presence
   over many miles with their cries,
E ndangered species, that we should protect,
   not capture for meat or for tricks,
S ave the whale, their future is in our hands
   not our sighs.

Emily Cutts-Watson (12)
Loreto Grammar School

MY CAT

My cat, Arthur, is a particular cat
He likes to make sure where he'll sit
He picks a spot on the bathroom chair
And begins his wash with great care.

Licks from his whiskers the last drop of sauce
And begins to wash his dainty paws
And when he's finished his daily chores
He needs to find a position to doze.

One paw there or one paw there?
He cannot decide, he doesn't know where
These hard decisions he has to make
Make up your mind for goodness sake!

Michaela Hoare (12)
Loreto Grammar School

WHO DO I WANT TO BE LIKE WHEN I GROW UP?

Who do I want to be like when I grow up? I was asked the other day.
I thought about it for a while and realised I didn't have a clue.
Maybe I'll be like my hero, Michael Owen, and play football.
Yeah, the first female player on an all-male team.

No, maybe I'll be like Jennifer Aniston, a TV star and film actress.
Or maybe when I grow up I'll be like Calvin Klein:
A fashion designer and multimillionaire just for designing
a few items of clothing.

Who do I want to be like when I grow up? I was asked the other day.
I want to be like Neil Armstrong and travel into space.
Or even a highly talented animator of children's cartoons.
Maybe when I grow up I will be like a Spice Girl:
A very talented and successful female singer married to an
equally successful footballer.

But then I realised whatever I do, I know exactly
Who I want to be like most of all:
The person I know best, *me!*

Emma Shiel (13)
Loreto Grammar School

THE LION

As he prowls along the dusty road,
searching for his prey.
He looks to his left and looks to his right,
but nothing is there today.
The clouds cover the sun,
the lion turns to run.

Natalie McGrath (13)
Loreto Grammar School

PEPPER

I'm in a dark room in a very dark house,
There is no noise, not even the stir of a mouse.
I'm thinking of Pepper the pony I once had,
Even now when I think of him, I feel very sad.

How will I stop this sorrow? How will I fight the pain?
I really, really miss him, I'll say that again and again.
I suppose we had to sell him, I just couldn't cope,
I didn't know if he'd throw me off, I just had to hope.

I've said I really miss him, I think of him all the time,
I've got to go to sleep now, so this is the end of the rhyme.
I'm still in this room in this very dark place,
I miss Pep's body and I miss Pep's face.

Katharine Nichols (12)
Loreto Grammar School

THE BLACK RHINO

B ig and bold I roam the plain.
L onging for peace.
A lways afraid for my life.
C an't you see the harm?
K illing us for our horn.

R egal and strong.
H unters harassing us.
I   n danger, all the time.
N owhere to hide.
O nly death for us.

Joanne Hunt (12)
Loreto Grammar School

Elongated Cat

I have an elongated cat
He can be thin, he can be fat
He curls up in a nice round ball
You cannot see his head at all

I have an elongated cat
He has two pointed ears that
Show his feelings and twist around
To pick up every little sound

I have an elongated cat
He can be thin, he can be fat
He cleans himself with his rough pink tongue
Then lies on my bed stretched out long.

Christine Farmer (12)
Loreto Grammar School

A Child's Game

War is just a child's game,
The weapons being his toys,
His war field is just a burnt-out playground,
In which he 'plays' with other boys.

The cavalry horse he rides in war,
Is just a tattered slide,
And in this deadly burnt-out playground,
A thousand childish men have died.

Philippa Scaife (12)
Loreto Grammar School

NINE LIVES

Never before has my cat shown his claw,
But in a fit of rage he scratched the door,
Nine lives he had,
Now only eight,
As we bundled him out of the gate.

Various deeds took care of seven, six, five and four,
Leaving only three more, until I found,
His head sticking out of my dad's bed,
Yes, you have guessed it, he messed it,
Which took care of two more.

Now one life he has left, which is precious,
And must be kept,
Gone are all his ploys, he has stopped playing with my toys,
After all nine minus eight is one,
And I am glad he has not gone.

Tessa Keegan (12)
Loreto Grammar School

ELEPHANTS

E lephants, elephants how I love them,
L arge and wrinkly, heavy and wide,
E lephants they come in every size,
P lenty in the African forests,
H arassed by the hunters of the nation,
A frican, Indian, I do not mind,
N o more killing these wonderful beasts,
T hen they'll be free to roam, and feel at ease.

Naomi Robson (12)
Loreto Grammar School

WISHING

I wish I could taste a glimpse of moonlight
or the shimmering stars in the night sky.
I would like to race over the vast, gleaming rainbow.
I wish I had the freedom, the freedom of a butterfly
fluttering in the summer breeze.
I wish I could feel the anger and hatred inside of people
and soothe their burning rage.
I wish I could feel loved, knowing that someone would
always be there caring and looking out for me.
I would like to smell the sweetness of happiness and excitement.
I wish I could be lazy and watch the world go slowly by
or sit gazing at an endless, sandy beach, thinking, dreaming,
dreaming of a day when this might actually come true,
maybe one day, one day in heaven.

Victoria Dolan (13)
Loreto Grammar School

AN AEROPLANE

A sky soarer,
A far traveller,
A people transporter,
A cloud cruiser,
A high flier,
A time zone traveller,
A holidaymaker,
An airborne work place,
A service provider,
A supersonic streaker.

Rebecca Newsham (12)
Loreto Grammar School

My Poem

M is for a Merry Christmas to you.
E is early up in the morning to open presents.
R is for roast dinner on Christmas Day.
R is for red noses in the cold weather.
Y is for yes, it's Christmas again.

C is for Christmas cake we love to eat.
H is for holly on the trees.
R is for Rudolph the red-nosed reindeer.
I   is for icing on the cake.
S is for stocking which is hanging on my bed.
T is for turkey, yum yum.
M is marvellous presents we have received.
A is for Advent which leads us to Christmas.
S   is for surprises that we love to receive.

But most of all Merry Christmas means the
Celebration of *our Saviour to all.*

Catherine Gibbons (12)
Loreto Grammar School

My Dog

A lazy lounger
A tail wagger
A ball catcher
A loyal companion
A hungry muncher
A bouncing barker
A cheeky chomper
A slobbery sleeper.

Ruth Lavelle (12)
Loreto Grammar School

FRIEND

'Friend'. What does 'friend' mean?
Is it something that can never be seen?
Is it something to look for, to seek?
Will I discover a 'friend' next week?

Is a 'friend' something to drink?
Do you wash one up at the sink?
How do I know where to find one?
Am I too late? Have they all gone?

What was that? What did you say?
You said I can find a 'friend' now, today?
All I have to do is join in, just be me?
You could have told me before,
That's all I needed, you see!

Hello everyone! How are all of you?
Would you like to come with me and visit the zoo?
I'd like to be friends with everyone!
Yes everyone, everyone under the sun!

Alexa Morton (13)
Loreto Grammar School

SQUIRREL

A noisy nibbler,
A quick climber,
A sneaky scamperer,
A nut nicker,
A bristly coated,
Bushy tailed,
Part of wildlife.

Roisin Dooley (11)
Loreto Grammar School

I'M TRYING TO WRITE A POEM

I'm trying to write a poem, I'm trying very hard,
Rhyming words and complicated verses,
Iambic pentameter and quick reverses,
Similes and metaphors, not to mention comic pause,
Enjambement too, now let's see,
What rhymes with doors and chimney?
Commas and colons, personification too,
What's the subject matter? Nothing too taboo!
I'm trying to write a poem from deep down in my heart,
I can't,
I can't,
I can't get it right,
I simply cannot see the light.
I'm trying to write a poem,
Oh yeah, at last I got it right.

Sarah Lindsay (12)
Loreto Grammar School

IT'S MY HAMSTER

A dull coloured
Lettuce eater
A nasty nipper
A greedy gremlin
A fluff ball
A flower eater
A sharp eyed sleeper
A lazy lodger
A busybody.

Josephine O'Neill (11)
Loreto Grammar School

THE PIG

Little pink pig so small and sure
You eat so much and now want more
You roll in mud and squeal and play
That is your routine every day.

Little pink pig so small and stout
All you do is trundle about
Trundling here, trundling there
That's what you do everywhere

Little pink pig so small and fat
Why does your tail curl out like that?
Why is your dinner so big?
It's probably because you're a pig.

Keira Ring (12)
Loreto Grammar School

TERRY'S CHOCOLATE ORANGE

A tasty treat
An orange orb
A wrapped winner
A succulent smell
A slim segment
A creamy confection
A smooth surface
A rich, dark desire
A sweet temptation.

Claire Miller (11)
Loreto Grammar School

ROLLER-COASTER

Waiting, waiting in the line,
Is the scariest time of all,
Sweat is dripping down your brow,
Then when you climb into the cart,
You feel the pounding of your heart,
Then suddenly you're soaring high,
You were scared, you wonder why,
Up and down and loop the loop,
You're in the sky and flying high,
Now the biggest drop of all,
You tremble with excitement and fear,
You throw your arms up and call 'Weeeeeee!'
You get up trembling,
You've hit your side,
And go and queue for another ride.

Corrina O'Brien (12)
Loreto Grammar School

DUCK

A greedy eater
A graceful glider
A quick flyer
A strong plunger
A low swooper
A slow waddler
A noisy quacker.

Monica Jones (11)
Loreto Grammar School

THE SUN

I look at you but you blind me
I look at you without fear
I like the way you warm my back
But you really don't hear
When I sing to the clouds around you
When I talk to your stars at night
I know you'll never answer
But what you do is give me light
The moon is lit at night by you
At dawn you show yourself
To the world you watch by day
Which needs you to keep its health
But you sometimes hide behind the clouds
You sometimes give us a fright
You even sometimes dry our waters
But I love your wonderful light.

Caroline Rushton (12)
Loreto Grammar School

A PLANT

Rustling leaves,
roots very long,
colour attracts bees in the summer,
makes the garden gleam.
With its colour so bright,
they'll always survive the *night,*
in their little coloured pots.

Lisa Feldhahn (11)
Loreto Grammar School

HUNTER OF THE SKIES

Gliding high,
Up, up in the sky.
Its wings spread out,
Far and wide.
Its body floating
On the air.
Its tail steering
Everywhere.

Looking for prey
Down below,
It spots a fish
Squirming in the sea.
Quick as a flash
It scoops it up
Trapped in its claw,
Life ends.

Such a meal this will provide,
For the hunter of the skies.

Lucy Rowe (12)
Loreto Grammar School

SALLY THE SPIDER

There was once a spider called Sally,
Who lived with her brother named Barry.
They lived in a web,
Spun finely with thread,
Which was made down a very dark alley.

Katy Gorman (12)
Loreto Grammar School

I LIE IN MY BED

At night I lie in my bed
Mum comes and tucks me in
'Are there any ghosts?' I ask
Mum smiles a funny grin
'Don't be silly Gemma dear
There's no such thing as ghosts'
'Then why can I see one flying past the lamp post?'
'Go off to sleep,' she sneaked out of the door.

I lie there still and with a chill
I can see that monster behind the door
It's coming towards me, 'Help' I cry
Mum rushes in and with a sigh
Says I can sleep in her bed.

Gemma McDermott (12)
Loreto Grammar School

A RABBIT

A cute ball.
Floppy ears.
Small feet.
A little pouncer.
A furry jumper.
Grass eater.
Outdoor animal.
Round brown eyes.

Erin Kilheeney (11)
Loreto Grammar School

THE PANTHER

His sleek, black coat glistened in the light,
That the moon threw down on the jungle.
What are the deep thoughts looming inside this
Mystical and mysterious animal,
Watching and waiting,
Watching and waiting?

In his eyes are a glimmer,
A glimmer that represents courage and wisdom,
Of skill and ability.
He stretches out on his branch like a king on his throne,
Watching and waiting,
Watching and waiting.

He is terrifying, yet elegant,
Speechless but proud.
He is the wizard weaving the magic in the deep of the night,
Watching and waiting,
Watching and waiting.

Colette Flynn (11)
Loreto Grammar School

A TIGER

A fierce creature
A wild wildcat
A great hunter
An orange gleaming coat
Almighty claws
A scary growl
A long swishing tail
An endangered species.

Abigail Renshaw (11)
Loreto Grammar School

LEAVES

The leaves in the dusty street,
Fly into one big heap.
All colours - yellow, brown and red,
They have fallen off the trees and are now dead.
As winter draws near all the leaves have gone,
And all the frost creeps upon,
The trees that only have branches.
Now it's near summer,
And the leaves are blooming in colour,
Almost every shade of green.
They do not fall off,
As they are new and lush,
And new flowers are very near.

Hannah Pond (12)
Loreto Grammar School

A FOUNTAIN PEN

An ink writer
A thin rubber
An elegant pattern
A cartridge drinker
A lid bearer
A paper roller
A paper coverer.

Sophie Williams (11)
Loreto Grammar School

THE TIGER

I saw the tiger
creeping slowly through
the forest looking for
its prey.

The tiger listens very
carefully then a twig
snaps not that far away.

Then a rodent runs in
to its trap, the tiger
pounces for a very
nice snack.

Jennifer Moore
Loreto Grammar School

EXTINCTION

O bservant, kind faces emerge from the leaves
R uler of the forest, king of the trees.
A gain a plea from beasts, 'We don't get a say.'
N ature never meant it to end this way.
G rim baby faces in anxious despair
U nder protection of mother's strong arms.
T he lonesome male, his thoughts occupy him
A t a sure advantage men undermine him.
N o sign of life, hunting, playing. Silence reigns.

Lizzie Walsh (12)
Loreto Grammar School

TIMMY'S MONSTER

'Go off to bed,' Timmy's mum said,
and this is something Tim hates.
For under his bed,
lives a monster called Fred,
and under his bed Fred waits.

He's got red eyes,
and big green hair
and when Tim looks under
he gives him a scare!
He makes the bed creak,
and snores in the night
while poor Tim sits there
shivering with fright.

Sian Clancy (13)
Loreto Grammar School

SCAREDY CAT

He creeps slowly and silently,
Through the old house he will go,
For outside there are footprints,
Footprints in the snow.

It's deserted, he thinks,
Creak goes the old house.
It's just the wind, he thinks,
Or maybe . . . a mouse.

Jodi Carroll Old (12)
Loreto Grammar School

SNOW

Snow, snow,
Watch it glow,
Watch it tumble,
Watch it flow.
It falls from the sky,
Way up high,
And lands on the floor,
In front of my door.
Snow, snow, snow.

Snow, snow,
How hard does it blow?
It comes from the west,
To where it looks best,
And lies on the ground,
Like a sleeping hound.
Snow, snow, snow.

Snow, snow,
It lies on show.
It tickles my nose,
And chills my toes.
The tips of my fingers are freezing cold,
Because the tips of my gloves are very old.
Snow, snow, snow.

Snow, snow,
It's nearly time to go,
Mother is calling me, to taste her dough.
The snowman I made, stands up bold,
His face friendly, but yet cold.
Snow, snow, snow.

Rebecca Teresa Carroll (12)
Loreto Grammar School

THE GOLDFISH-SHARK

He told us Tim was a very rare species
of goldfish, from Mongolia in fact.
We all liked the look of him, fin and all,
so we took him and didn't look back.

We thought that it was rather odd,
when auntie's arm got rather thin,
with nibble marks along the side,
we didn't see Tim's evil grin.

When we were eating Sunday dinner,
we were none the wiser,
when our bratty cousin's finger went
(still, we always did despise her.)

And when mum's 1lb Christmas steak
went missing, (still frozen and raw)
and when the trail led to Tim's own bowl
well - that was the final straw!

We took him back, but the owner had moved
I don't think he wanted Tim back,
so we threw him in the nearest pond
and that was the end of that.
        Phew!

Rosie Davies (11)
Loreto Grammar School

CHARLIE

I have a young kitten called Charlie,
He will eat anything including barley,
He'll stand on your head,
And sleep on your bed,
And his mother's name is Carlie.

I have a young kitten called Charlie,
He used to live in a place near Darley,
He has a cute nose,
And he bites my toes,
And his brother's name is Marley.

Sinéad Hosty (12)
Loreto Grammar School

BONFIRE NIGHT

The flames are soaring up to the sky,
The ashes spurting out in the nigh,
The fireworks blasting,
They're everlasting,
Lighting up the dark, dull sky.

Children playing and running about,
The fireworks surely defeat their shout,
Sparklers waving in the air,
Parents stand and watch with care,
Smoke on their clothes and smoke in their hair,
Fireworks, fireworks everywhere.

Blasting up high in the sky,
Making pretty patterns up they fly,
Spinning, swirling, blasting out with glee,
Soon ashes they will be,
The fireworks keep going on and on.

The bonfire is burning out,
The finale is here and that's no doubt,
The final firework raises up to the sky,
The spurts of light and bursts of joy,
A musty smell takes over the air,
The night is over, there is no more to share.

Louise Mosley (12)
Loreto Grammar School

GOLD

Gold, gold,
It's a funny thing,
It's only a metal,
But a valuable thing.

Gold, gold,
It must be quite old,
It's been going on for centuries,
So I am told.

It sparkles and twinkles,
And glitters and shines,
It must be the prettiest thing
That I can find.

Rachel Mugford (12)
Loreto Grammar School

MIAOW, MIAOW

Miaow, miaow says the cat
Go and sit on your mat
You're fat and lazy, black and crazy
Don't dare jump on me, I feel hazy

Miaow, miaow says the cat
Go and chase that big brown rat
You are a lazy fat puss
Now don't make a fuss
Get out from your hide
Or I'll tan your backside.

Erica Mousah (12)
Loreto Grammar School

HAPPY FAMILIES

Now when you see my family and me we look like a happy family,
but it doesn't last long and everything goes wrong.
Now the neighbours must think we are a rowdy lot, slamming doors
and shouting a lot, but we are not always like that, no!
Most of the time we are a happy family, that's when mum is not
shouting at dad for burning the tea and when my sisters are not having
a wrestling fight or running riot late at night.
No, we are quite the civilised type except for when we go partying
on New Year's Eve night.
Now our house is a mad house and that's how it's always been.
Once the outside of our house was surrounded by rats, we even have
a dog who is scared of black bin bags, but believe it or not we are a
happy family, no matter what it may seem.

Claire Farrell (12)
Loreto Grammar School

CHRISTMAS TIME

Christmas time is so exciting,
Christmas time is so much fun,
With presents waiting around the tree,
Oh! And it's only just begun.

Candles burning tall and bright,
The flames quiver and curl all through the night,
Will he come? Oh yes, he might,
Go to sleep now, curl up tight.

He's up there now going from roof to roof,
With all of his reindeer travelling on hoof.

Elizabeth Kirk (12)
Loreto Grammar School

ANSWER

Answer, answer what's the answer?
Shall I just pretend that I'm a dancer?
I look around the classroom and plea,
Please, please help me!

Answer, answer, what's the answer?

The teacher's waiting, staring at me,
Shall I just turn around and flee?
Shall I just take a chance,
I turn around and I glance.

Answer, answer, what's the answer?

Panic-stricken, in shock, in fear,
I know the answer's very near,
But what is it, I just need to think,
The teacher's looking at me and,
Gives me a wink.

Answer, answer, what's the answer?

I've got it, I've got, I've got it at last,
But I don't know has my chance passed?
I tell the teacher, a pleasing look,
As he writes it down in his book.

Answer, answer, I know the answer.

Sarah Finney (12)
Loreto Grammar School

GHOSTS

Ghosts are everywhere in the night,
Ghosts are everywhere giving people a fright,
Ghosts can float,
Ghosts can scare,
There are a lot of ghosts out at the dark fair.

Ghosts are said to have unfinished business to do,
Which sometimes includes going boo, boo, boo,
Some people don't believe in ghosts,
And some people do, do, do.

At night in the dark they are whirling around,
We can't see them, because they're not on the ground,
I really wish I could see a ghost,
Maybe my great grandma at my bedpost.

Leanne Ogden (12)
Loreto Grammar School

WINTER!

It was a cold winter's day and it was snowing,
And the wind was blowing,
And the brook was flowing,
And trees were showing their bare branches.

On that cold winter's day I was full of cheer,
For Christmas was near,
To be with loved ones so dear,
At this special time of the year.

Rachael Tyler (13)
Loreto Grammar School

STORMY NIGHT

The dark clouds moved over the sea,
Rumbling, rumbling near.
The seagulls flew away from the shore,
Their eyes all filled with fear.

The rumbling clouds moved
Towards the cities,
People running in every direction,
Searching around for an umbrella,
And opening it up for protection.

The farmers closed their windows,
As darkness crept over the town.
The darkening clouds moved over the country,
Making all the animals frown.

Then everything was silent,
And the rumbling suddenly stopped
And then there was a little bang,
As though all the clouds had popped.

And then it came pouring down
Like a sheet of glass,
Wrapping everything in its clutches,
The buildings, the trees, the grass.

The rain fell down like cats and dogs,
Pitter-patter, pitter-patter,
And the town was engulfed in fog,
Pitter-patter, pitter-patter.

Natalie Mason (13)
Loreto Grammar School

THE KING OF THE JUNGLE

He's the King of the Jungle, and how he likes to roar,
And no matter how much he eats, he's always back for more.
He plods along gently yet proudly and tall,
For he's the King of the Jungle, but that's not all.

He's got a sandy coloured body and a sandy fluffy mane,
But despite his sweet appearance, he is really quite a pain.
You can see his teeth when he roars and his great humungous paws,
With a gobble and a gulp he'll swallow them whole.
They'll find themselves inside him, even the tiny mole,
Now off he goes back to his pride, while the other animals try to hide.
For they know he'll be back for the rest of them,
For soon he will be hungry again.

Tamsin Brown (11)
Loreto Grammar School

GUMBLEGORE

Deep in the forest, amongst the trees,
Down in the woods is where Gumblegore breathes.
Powerful claws and a long, bushy tail,
Green eyes enough to make a strong man frail.
Fierce as a bulldog, roars like a lion,
Huge strong arms with muscles of iron.
The ground gives a rumble when he jumps from his lair,
People are so scared of him, they're filled with despair.

Everything about him makes you pale with fright,
That's the Gumblegore monster in the dead of the night!

Sarah Kay (11)
Loreto Grammar School

THE SISTER

Sisters can be annoying
Sisters can be fun
Most people will agree with me
Go on, ask anyone.

She'll help you with your homework
And answer all your sums
And before you can say anything
You two are the best of chums

But when you get home from school
You shan't have any choice
As when you are at tea with mother
She'll announce in a big loud voice:
'Oh sister, why weren't you at orchestra today?'
Then you'll feel small
About one centimetre tall
And have nothing at all to say

Now, forget what I said earlier
And listen to the rest
For now I'm speaking truthfully
My sister is the best.

Eva D Krysiak (12)
Loreto Grammar School

STARRY NIGHT

The stars shone in the dark night sky,
the night was cold and silent,
the haunted night gave out a cry,
the wind was sharp and violent.

The wind rustled the leaves on the trees,
the stars shone at a height.
I stared at the stars, down on my knees,
on that one starry night.

Yasmin Fletcher (12)
Loreto Grammar School

WAR

The shouts, the screams,
the aftermath dreams.
Thousands of men fight,
a handful survive.
Half slaughtered at night.
What was their drive?

Vietnam, D-Day,
all down to our selfish way.
Wanting what is not ours,
leads to all these lifelong scars.

You sit waiting,
you hear a gunshot.
Holding in your hating,
while the Captain begins to plot.
'Jones, forward. Smith, here!'
You try to conquer your inevitable fear.

Couldn't we settle this like
civilised beings?
Save the bloodshed and the pain.
Please O Lord, don't let it
begin again.

Danielle Gray (13)
Loreto Grammar School

CATS

Cats are mysterious animals in many different ways
They lie around and sleep quite sound
For most of the day
And then at night when we're asleep the cats are out to play
And when we wake they like to sleep
They only stop to stretch and get a bite to eat
The way they bend with such ease
And always land on their feet
Is rather different you can see
From humans like you and me
They are agile, sleek and swift
They run like shadows in the mist
They jump with such elegance and grace
They hunt for mice and birds to eat
Their eyes and coats glisten in light
You cannot guess what a cat is thinking
From the expression on its face
So I think I'm right in saying that cats are
Mysterious animals in many different ways.

Melissa Chaaya (12)
Loreto Grammar School

I LIKE THE SEA!

I like to go down to the sea
To wade in as far as I dare
I like to go really deep
Till the spray is splashing my hair
I like the sea

I like to jump the waves
But not when I land on a rock
I like to duck down in the sea
And swim around just me
I like the sea

I like to let my feet sink into the sand
I like to swirl them round and round
And make a splashing sound
I like the sea

I like to play ball in the sea
But the sea doesn't always play with me
The tide drags the ball away
But other days allow me to play
I like the sea.

Fiona Clair Mackey (12)
Loreto Grammar School

ALONE

I find my mind when I'm alone,
No screaming children or ringing telephone.
My solitude is what keeps me alive,
It lets all my fantasies and dreams thrive.
I can slip away to some far off land,
Or lie in the sun, on the golden sand.

I realise this place is not real,
But I can reach my conscience and see how I feel.
The mind is a neighbourhood,
Behind every door: bad or good!
Every door holds a secret thought,
All the truth I ever sought.

Away from stress and anxiety,
With no rules and commands; I am free.
How I long to be alone,
Get to know the real me,
In a place where dreams become reality.

Suzanne Hunt (14)
Loreto Grammar School

I WISH I WAS

I wish I was a bird,
to fly in the sky.
First stooping low,
then gliding high.

I wish I was a flower,
to be a bud in May.
Then open my lovely petals,
so that you can point and say . . .

I wish I was a squirrel,
to climb in a tree.
No in fact I am just glad,
I am just glad I'm me.

Charlotte McDonnell (13)
Loreto Grammar School

RED

Red is the sunset shimmering in the light
Red is a fire burning with all its might
Red is an engine storming through town
To rescue a house that's quickly burning down
Red is a beetroot that I hate to eat
Red is my colour when I've tripped over my feet
Red is anger when you are mad
When you're unhappy, when you are sad
Red is United, the best team of all
Red is the postbox in the shopping mall
Red are the tomatoes fresh from the store,
Mum's just eaten them so we need to buy more.

Erin Dooley (13)
Loreto Grammar School

DON'T WORRY

The important exam tomorrow,
Will I ever remember this lot?
When was the Battle of Hastings?
When was the Gunpowder Plot?
I remembered what mum said,
'Don't worry'

Oh! I can't eat my breakfast,
Queen Elizabeth keeps coming to mind,
My stomach is turning and churning,
When was the Magna Carta signed?
I remembered what mum said,
'Don't worry'

My knees are knocking nervously,
As I stand in the line,
I must think about Henry VIII,
How many wives did he kill?
I remembered what mum said,
'Don't worry'

Tudors and Stuarts keep coming to mind,
It's time to turn the paper over,
My heart is pounding fast,
I wish I could get up and run away,
I remembered what mum said,
'Don't worry'

Suddenly a switch has been turned on,
A bright light flashes in my mind!
Oliver Cromwell and Queen Elizabeth . . .
All my facts and dates I can find,
What did mum say?
I can't remember!

Jemma Williams (13)
Loreto Grammar School

THE SEASONS

Winter is here,
I walk along the garden path
Wrapped up from head to toe
My nose, a tap dripping
But I can't turn it off
Feet disappear in snow
Cat scratches at the door

Suddenly step into spring
Start shedding hat, coat and gloves
Trees full of little tiny buds
A twitter from a bird
Sets the flock off
The cat spies on its prey

Stroll into a warm summer breeze
I skip, I jump, I hop
The buzzing of the awaiting wasps
Shouts from excited children
See springtime buds glisten
As they open into glorious flowers

Brisk, crisp leap into autumn
Return my coat to my back
Swaying of descending leaves
Cat curled up in the corner
Adults sweep leaves into bags
Finally, I reach my destination
What a long journey.

Elizabeth Moley (13)
Loreto Grammar School

FOOTBALL

I was running up the pitch
Had to get the ball
But as I slid in
I heard the ref call
'No two-footed challenges, I don't know what you think
But you deserve a yellow card and you stink'
The match ended 1:0
To us I mean
I scored the winning goal
It's only because I stole
Someone else's goal
I pretended to tap it in
So for leading scorer I'd win.

Leah Thomas (11)
Loreto Grammar School

CHOCOLATE

A dangerous treat
A delicious venom
A dentist's delight
A sweet, sugary scoundrel
A delightful decision
A plentiful platter
A mouth-watering morsel
The food of addiction
A creamy comfort.

Katie Grace (11)
Loreto Grammar School

WAITING

Waiting, waiting for the door to open,
I can hear the silent thudding of her footsteps.
She is approaching nearer,
But I can no longer hear her.
I have been enclosed in my own mind.

Waiting, waiting for the door to open,
For the small plump lady to announce the news.
Will it be pleasant or maybe just painful?
I only have a few minutes to find out.

Waiting, waiting for the door to open,
Is there someone really there?
Footsteps, footsteps getting louder,
Now I'm getting really scared.

Waiting, waiting for the door to open,
Expecting a sudden swish of air,
But there is no squeak of hinges,
Why is the door just sitting there?

Waiting, waiting for the door to open,
Oh no, the news is bad.
How am I going to cope with this?
Well, I already have.

Laura Gooch (13)
Loreto Grammar School

THE FROG

The frog in the pond sits on a log
with the sun peering through the trees.
Many others are with him,
butterflies, dragonflies, birds and bees.

Hopping from one lily pad to another,
his camouflage keeps him under cover.
His big round eyes that shine so bright,
looking for a mate he croaks in the night.

Soft slippery, and damp is his skin,
no other frog's quite like him.
His long tongue catches his snack,
so flies watch out he may attack.

Katie Gyves (11)
Loreto Grammar School

THE DOLPHIN

Splash! The dolphin dives
Through the waters with the tide
The sound of music, the dance begins
The fish are dancing, wriggling their fins
The music stops, the sea is quiet
Something happens to start a riot
A power boat goes roaring by
The dolphin lets out an anguished cry
As fast as lightning it flees away
To calmer waters miles away.

Maria Thompson (11)
Loreto Grammar School

FEARS

I hear a creak upon the stairs
and I am afraid that it might be a bunch of bears.
I'm frightened of the night
and of the dark,
I'm even afraid of a dog that barks.
I hear the creak once again
and I can hear it getting closer,
but I'm sure that it isn't my sister Samosa.
Ah it is her, oh it's all right
but she did give me a real good fright.

I see someone in my room
flying on a kitchen broom.
He has disappeared.
Oh where can he be?
If it wasn't for the darkness, I would be able to see.
Oh no don't take me away
just go away and leave me alone
and please don't turn me into a garden gnome.
Oh it was just a bird
that left me quivering at the knee
I left the window open you see.

Oh how can I ever get to sleep
knowing that I could be attacked
at any moment once I've turned my back?
I hear a slither in the distance,
I try to scream, and I try to yell,
but nothing can save me from this hell.

There's no chance to live,
but I try to run
and I am then awoken by the sound of a gun.
I look around
there's nothing there,
so I snuggle down with my big stuffed bear.

Helen Doyle (13)
Loreto Grammar School

IT'S A DOG'S LIFE!

I really don't see why I should slog,
Through that muddy field,
Don't call *me* a neurotic dog,
Would *you* traipse through that bog?

They feed me this gunk called Pedigree Chum,
And out of a tin, as well,
Honestly, would *they* eat something,
That had such an awful smell?

They say I'm a poor guard dog,
I'd like to see *them* try,
I wake up at seven every morning,
And wait for the postman to arrive.

They gave me something called a dog basket,
When I chewed it up, you should have heard them yell,
They set the children on me,
I thought I was in hell!

Those humans are pathetic,
They won't even let me chew,
They treat me like an *animal*,
Don't they know I'm a pedigree shih tzu?

Aisling O'Driscoll (13)
Loreto Grammar School

THE SIX WIVES OF HENRY VIII

Catherine of Aragon was the first,
but things just went from bad to worse.
Next in line was Anne Boleyn,
didn't like her, did her in.
Jane Seymour followed on,
but before long poor Jane was gone.
Anne of Cleves the Flanders mare,
pretty soon she wasn't there.
Then along came Catherine Howard,
but before long that marriage soured.
By now the priests' throats were getting hoarse,
when Catherine proved Parr for the course.

Jennifer Ann Simister (11)
Loreto Grammar School

FRIENDS

Friends will laugh with you when you are happy.
They will cheer you up when you are sad.
Friends will make you feel better when you're feeling bad.
They may ask you to join in their games.
Introduce you to new people and tell you all their names.
Friends will save you a place in the dinner queue.
They should always, always stick up for you.
Your friends might just joke and have a laugh.
Or they may invite you to the local swimming bath.
Without our friends, what would we do?
Friends are here to look after
        you!

Eve Barry (11)
Loreto Grammar School

THE BLACK CAT

Late one dark and wintry night,
A creature of ebony coat,
Four delicate legs, feet tinged with white,
Strode down a road, grey and remote,
She moved with caution lest a beast,
A natural enemy of hers,
Should spy her fragile frame with ease,
If caught, then she'd be cursed.

But her silent stride was of no avail,
For her predator's silhouette,
Stood mighty in the moonlight pale,
A mouth baring ivory teeth made her fret,
Her feeble form faltered at the sight before her,
She withdrew to a corner nearby,
Her horrored heart beating like a jack hammer,
Knowing if she didn't flee, she'd die.

She ran as far as her legs would allow,
Behind heard the plodding paws,
Of her evil enemy clear and loud,
And of course his spine-chilling roars,
She fled for her life and on through the night,
Galloped with all her might,
In the last moments of her strife,
The poor creature was caught . . . and paid the price.

Frances Morgan (12)
Loreto Grammar School

THE PIG WHO COULDN'T SING

There was a pink pig who was very big,
he didn't really care about a thing,
he would sit at home alone,
chatting on the phone,
the only thing he wanted was to sing.

He would stay inside the house,
practising his pounce,
to catch the big fat mouse
which was stuck inside the house.
However hard he tried,
he couldn't catch a fly,
so the tired pig cried,
and went to sulk inside the sty.

The pig was getting bored,
he couldn't catch the mouse,
he didn't know a thing
and the pig still couldn't sing.

Winter came, the pig was cold,
the mouse was frozen, yet alive
and getting old.

How the pig tried to get his voice alive,
but however hard he tried,
he couldn't get it right, so the pig cried.
The pig and the mouse became friends,
they said we'll see it through till the end.
The pig got in a show, the mouse didn't know how
because the pig didn't know a thing,
and the pig still couldn't sing.

Nicola Furniss (12)
Loreto Grammar School

THEY'VE LEFT ME WITH NO ONE!

I've come home to find an empty house,
There is no noise, not even a mouse.
I look around, but just to find.
A house with no one, no one inside.

I hear no voices of people telling tales,
Or laughing and giggling over the balcony rails.
I start to sweat,
As I think what has happened.
They've taken away everyone,
And left me with no one, no one inside.

I hear the phone ring,
And I think should I answer?
I walk up slowly and pick up the receiver,
But then I realise the wrong I have done.
There is no voice on the other end,
Just a small whisper saying,
'We've left you with no one, no one inside.'

What have they done?
Is everyone dead?
Or are they coming,
To catch me instead?
What should I do?
I can hear someone knocking,
And the sound of someone far away saying,
'They've left you with no one, no one inside.'

Siobhan Lillie (13)
Loreto Grammar School

THE ELEPHANT

He lives in the back garden,
But sometimes he wanders about.
He steals things out of my bedroom,
With his big grey snout.

I bought some orange nail varnish,
That was only yesterday.
And then I saw him with it on,
He said, 'It's to brighten up my grey!'

He's always stealing things off me,
He stole my new hairspray.
And when I asked him why he'd done it,
He said 'I was having a bad hair day.'

So I thought I'd get my own back,
You know for all the things he'd taken.
For all the new things that I'd bought,
For all the cakes I'd baken,

Everything I owned he stole,
It would be OK if he'd only asked.
But no, he doesn't do anything like that,
That's why I did this devious task.

One day when he lay sleeping,
I took my permanent pens.
I scribbled all over his body,
And took a picture through my lens.

But I'd forgotten one minor detail,
One little, well, quite big thing.
This elephant loved bright colours,
He said they encouraged him to sing.

So now every night when I go to bed,
He sings tunes by 'All Saints'.
Or sometimes mimics 'Boyzone',
Oh why didn't I use my washable paints?

Now he uses my money,
To place all his bets.
So I tell you now to remember this,
An elephant *never* forgets!

Christina Murphy (11)
Loreto Grammar School

HORSEFLY

I am a horsefly
My favourite meal's apple pie
I fly, I leap and I never go to sleep
I soar through the sky
With an ebony scenery behind me
The gravity pushes my strawberry-blond mane over my eye
I peer down to see where, for tonight I'll lie
As my feet touch the ground, I, mighty ruler of the sky
Lie upon the grass.

And now my learned friends you realise,
I am only a figment of your imagination . . .

Clare Rushton (12)
Loreto Grammar School

FIRST DAY AT SCHOOL

I was awake before the alarm,
Clothes all ready,
Bags all packed,
With my special lucky charm.

A brand new start,
A new leaf turned,
New friends perhaps,
I feel quite smart.

Maroon and blue,
Cream as well,
I'm so excited,
Worries are few.

But then I stop!
Outside the door,
A funny feeling,
Deep inside,
Nervous,
Excited,
I could have cried.

Felicity Woof (11)
Loreto Grammar School

IF ONLY I COULD . . .

If only I could be a parrot I'd fly away at night.
I might even be a conductor with a band of kangaroos
That's what I'd choose.

If only I could be a pig,
I'd get greedy and become fat.
There wouldn't be a living thing
To stop me, except a living cat. *Miaow.*

If only I could be a monkey
I'd dance all night
And my nickname would be Funky.

Last but not least, I'd like to become a cat
I'd rule above everybody
But alas how would I do all that?

Colette McGrory (12)
Loreto Grammar School

THE HUNTER

His beady eyes feast upon his prey,
As the night meets with the end of the day,
He crouches low, his ears flat,
His claws project about to attack,
Tail swaying, he slowly walks,
As the ill-trained hunter quietly stalks,
The adrenaline pumps,
His body swishes,
He pounces, jumps,
But clearly misses.

The victim was a leaf,
Which blew away,
That once alone,
And defenceless lay,
That vicious creature, a tiny kitten,
Although has failed, with pride is smitten,
His gentle miaow is heard at the door,
And the fallen hero is home once more.

Lauren Morell (13)
Loreto Grammar School

DOLPHIN

One day whilst swimming in the sea,
a beautiful dolphin passes me.
She says 'Hello! Why don't be shy, I'm not a shark,
I will not bite!'
As I reply,
she leaps into the sky,
then dives back in with a very long grin.
'Why don't you take a dive in with me into
the ocean and you will see
Big fat fish, small and tall, octopuses,
jellyfish and creatures that crawl.
There's a whole new world under the ocean,
which isn't full of this world's commotion!
So please come down, down with me and see
what a wonderful time there will be.'
'I'd love to come and see the waters so calm,
but I'm afraid without oxygen my body
will be caused harm!
So, I'm afraid I'll have to say goodbye,
being with you was fun that is no lie.
I will definitely come and visit you again sometime.'

Emma Stuart (13)
Loreto Grammar School

THE SCOTTISH MAN

The Scottish man, well my daddy,
Sat on the couch as a bonnie wee laddy.
He had a wee doggy, a bonnie wee lassie,
A brother called Peter, a sister called Cassie.
Five of them squashed in a tiny wee housey,
And a little black cat to chase away the wee mousey.

Caroline Dunne (13)
Loreto Grammar School

BONFIRE NIGHT!

Sparks and flames,
Bangs and cracks,
Bright colours fill the skies,
With laughter and goodbyes.

Children scream and adults shout,
Pets bark from morning till night.
Fire engines are all alert, waiting,
For the call from all who are hurt.

'Be careful,' we hear,
'Don't run around.
Just look in the sky,
And watch the colours go by.'

Helen Phillips (13)
Loreto Grammar School

CREATURE OF THE NIGHT

The cat is black and fierce
Its green eyes beginning to pierce
Coming out at night
When the world is rid of light
I watch and stare with awe
As the feline moves its jaw
And grabs a passing mouse
As I watch from the safety of my house.
As the sun starts to appear
The cat shows every sign of fear
And very soon the cat will be gone
But the memory goes on and on.

Victoria Stott (12)
Loreto Grammar School

WE'VE GOT A DOG

We've got a dog
And he's completely mad
He pulls the washing off the line
He's the stupidest dog we've had.

We've got a dog
He's just one big mistake
One day we took him for a walk
And he jumped straight in the lake.

He barks at the hairdryer
When his nose feels the warm breeze
He chases flies and tries to catch them
And barks at all the trees.

He jumps on all the couches
Covering them with hair
He lies on his back
With his legs stuck in the air.

We've got a dog
If he's walking anywhere
You can guarantee that it's because
There's some sort of food there.

We've got a dog
If you're thinking of calling him, don't
He's useless at his training
If you tell him to come he won't.

And if you're cooking in our house
You'd better be aware
That he'll jump up and lick the food
If you leave out a chair.

Whenever he sees a cat go past
And he does this with squirrels too
He gets really scared, he doesn't chase
As normal dogs are meant to do.

We've got a dog
And now you know
It'd be so much easier without him
But we wouldn't want him to go.

Catherine Hamilton (12)
Loreto Grammar School

HATE

I hate the way they crawl about,
slowly up the wall.
They have those little tiny legs,
that creep along the floor.

They sneak about around the house,
hiding in cracks and walls.
They have two legs here, and two legs there,
and all in all they have eight.

I would describe them as sly insects,
that spin webs all the time.
They catch a couple of flies a day,
and all I can do is wish they'd go away.

Spiders are my biggest fear,
as well as those slimy snakes.
I jump every time I see them come,
and run as fast as I can to my mum.

Jemma Cosgrove (13)
Loreto Grammar School

THE CROCODILE

The crocodile lay in his lair
waiting for his prey.
He lies there ever so still
wondering what it shall be today.

A bird, monkey or even a human
may enter the jaws of death.
The crunchy bones and juicy meat
may occupy his breath.

Oh what is that? A man ahead
he looks ever so tasty.
The crocodile flicks his tail and waits
for something tasty.

Thinking of a plan, to catch the tasty man
he jumps to his feet to savage the juicy meat.
The crocodile quickly thinks of something . . .

Snap! He's disappeared into the jaws of death,
he will never appear again.
Of course the crocodile will
snap and snap, again and again.

Katie Brown (12)
Loreto Grammar School

THE HAUNTED HOUSE

The smoky black house
The creak in the door
The shrill 'Ha, ha, ha'
That lives no more

The cry of the wolves
The dim of the light
They all come alive
In the dead of the night

The footsteps behind me
The crack on the wall
The death trap below me
Maybe I'll fall

I walk through the hallway
I stumble once more
Why did I bother
To come through that door?

Philippa Brown (13)
Loreto Grammar School

CONSTELLATIONS

Before the exploration of space, the moon and planets.
Man thought the heavens were the home and province
                                        of powerful gods.
They controlled not just the vast planet Earth,
                but the earthly fate of man himself.
And that the illustrations in the skies were powerful warnings.
And were the cause and reason for the human condition,
                        for the past and the future.

But in time man would place these gods with new gods
                        and new religions.
Who provide no greater or certain answers than those worshipped
                        by his Greek or Roman ancestors.
And now we seemed to have found certainties in science.
Believers all wait for a sign, a revelation.
Are our eyes turning skyward? Ready to accept the incredible.
We find our future and destiny written in the stars.
But how are we best to look, with new eyes or old?

Michelle Mullen (13)
Loreto Grammar School

ALONE

Alone in the house,
Oh no there's the phone!
Who could it be when I'm all on my own?
I turn on the telly to drown out the noise,
When all of a sudden I hear some boys.
They could break all the windows,
And kick down the door,
Strew all the furniture all over the floor.

I've gone all hot and sweaty,
My legs are like spaghetti,
I've never been so scared,
I feel like a rabbit who's snared,
I feel, I must confess,
I am a quivering mess.

A banging on the door,
Shakes me up even more,
Armed with a bat,
I creep as quiet as a cat,
Opening the door a crack,
And there before my eyes,
I have a great surprise,
I haven't been alone,
My mum was always home.

Bernadette Thompson (13)
Loreto Grammar School

IS THERE LIFE ON MARS?

Is there life on Mars?
I sometimes ask myself.
Maybe they shop at Cyber store
And take holidays to the moon.

Is there life on Mars?
My brother asked me once.
I said they'd come down one day
And eat him for their lunch.

Is there life on Mars?
I ask myself again
I thought do they have Earth bars
Just the same as we have Mars?

Louise Daley (12)
Loreto Grammar School

THE CANDLESTICK

I'm long and slender and sometimes slouch
Be careful if you touch me, *ouch!*
I'm red and blue and green and pink
And in the breeze I dance and wink.
You see me on a birthday cake
To count the years for birthday's sake.
I have a warm and glowing flame
I wonder if you've guessed my name.
My holder sometimes has a handle,
I'm wax and wick and called a candle.

Christine Armstrong (13)
Loreto Grammar School

BUSBY BEAR

I have a little teddy bear,
His name is Busby Brown,
He's small, sweet and cute,
And fits in the pocket of my dressing gown.

Busby has a button nose,
And brown eyes for you to see,
He wears a little red T-shirt,
Which Granny made for me.

I often wonder,
What Busby does at night,
Does he play with his teddy friends,
Or does he play with his kite?

I once lost Busby,
In the local store,
I found him under the magazines,
Which were near the stock room door.

Busby is my best friend,
There is no one else for me,
We go around together,
As happy as can be.

Rachel Taylor (13)
Loreto Grammar School

HIPPOPHANT

I'm a hippophant, I'm red and green
So at night I can easily be seen
I drink green water and eat blue trees
Ants and humans make me sneeze.

I'm a Hippophant I live in the blue tree wood
I don't know how to read and write
But if I tried I could.

I'm a Hippophant, I'm only eleven
I've been alone since I was seven
I like the morning dew
And I wouldn't be alive without you
I look real it may seem
But I'm only a part of this lovely dream.

Joanne Grant (11)
Loreto Grammar School

WE ARE WHAT WE ARE

I open my eyes and I really despise
that fact that I go to school.
If I was the Head
I'd be jolly instead
of the ones that make detention a rule.
The teachers just don't understand,
that us students who rule the land
are what we are
by far and by far
and the rest of the rules should be banned.

Homework, it just isn't right
I think we should have a free night.
If the teachers were there
and they knew the despair
then everything would turn out all right.

For the teachers that *did* understand
would think 'Oh this rule should be banned
for the pupils are right,
homework just isn't nice
in the meantime we'll give them a hand.'

Helen Sweeney (13)
Loreto Grammar School

GOODBYE MATTHEW

I saw you walking on a cloud,
At that moment I felt so proud,
But I knew that in my heart,
Even though we are gone we will never be apart.
Goodbye Matthew.

Every night I would have the same dream,
And every time it would seem so real,
You would return back into my heart,
But then you would leave and a new day would start.
Goodbye Matthew.

I love to see your sweet smile,
Looking down on me, it would shine a mile,
You got my attention with your charms,
Now I just want to be in your arms.
Goodbye Matthew.

Siobhan O'Grady (13)
Loreto Grammar School

MY TWO CATS

My cat Harold was black and white,
He was 12 years old and liked to roam throughout the day,
And come home at night,
He would run and pounce after silver balls,
He'd also grab your ankles with his paws.
He'd come and miaow for food,
And miaow to say thank you,
If he were in the mood.

My cat Misha,
Is tabby and white,
She likes to sneak around the house,
She also chases after mice,
She brought one home the other day,
As if it were a prize,
As she stared at me with her green, grey eyes.

Andrea Klikucs (12)
Loreto Grammar School

THE CROC AND I

As I walked into the jungle,
In the darkness of the night,
I glimpsed a small and shining light,
I walked a little closer and then I realised,
That there were two of them shining bright,

I peered into the darkness, the lights loomed closer,
I reached out to touch them,
But the velvet darkness of the night slipped through my fingers,
I stretched out my arm again and felt,
What was it? Scaly skin rough and wet,
What could it be? A snake, perhaps?

No, not a snake, too big for a snake,
I slithered my hand from snout to tail,
A crocodile snuggled and purred at me,
He grinned and growled and sat on my lap,
I rubbed his nose, he dare not snap,

He yawned, I yawned and fell asleep,
Dawn broke, I woke,
No croc anymore!

Victoria Briffa (12)
Loreto Grammar School

INSPIRATION

Sitting there,
Thinking,
Trying to find
Words for a poem
In my mind.

Wondering whether
It will ever be done,
So I can go out
And have some fun.

Oh what shall I write about?
What shall it be?
Write about others
Or write about me?

Wait a minute,
I have an idea,
To writing a whole poem
I am very near.

Inspiration was hard to find
But I finally managed
To write something that rhymed!

Aimée Beech (13)
Loreto Grammar School

A WONDER OR TWO

Pieces of land which surround the sea,
Seven of them for you and me,
There's Antarctica and Arctic, north and south,
North and South America that meet at the mouth.
There's Asia and Africa, Europe's where we live,
They're the continents, I've got nothing else to give.

Large triangles which surround the Earth,
They've been there since they were built at birth.
Great tombs are hidden deep inside,
If I'd told you they were small, I would have lied.
Inside the tombs Pharaohs lie dead,
Well preserved from toe to head.

Vanessa Rigby (12)
Loreto Grammar School

THE SEASONS

The brown and orange leaves,
Falling from the trees,
Little squirrels scurrying around,
Picking acorns up off the ground.
Preparing for their winter sleep,
Cosy and snug . . . zzz zzz.

The first of the winter snow appears,
The pitter-pattering is all I can hear,
The children are playing outside,
Throwing snowballs from side to side.

The snow stops and the sun comes out,
The spring sun warms up the air,
The baby rabbits jump about everywhere,
The baby birds are singing in their nests,
The mother birds have no rest.

The sun is shining bright and light,
The summer has come back,
Everything is warm and peaceful,
The summer is my favourite season.

Rebecca Wellock (12)
Loreto Grammar School

EARLY NIGHTS

Please let it be Saturday
I'm really tired
No not Monday
I'm really tired

She said early nights were what I needed
Her advice I should have heeded
Fiddled about till eleven at night
At nine I said I'd put out the light

I really am now paying the price
My heavy head, it doesn't feel nice
Honestly I'll be in bed for seven
The thought of it reminds me of heaven
But then seven comes and I forget
The promise I made I now regret
I fiddle about till eleven at night
Someone please put out the light

Please let it be Saturday
I'm really tired
No not Monday
I'm really tired.

Camilla Woof (13)
Loreto Grammar School

THE HAUNTED HOUSE

There it stood so big and tall
In the middle of the forest of nowhere.
The rain crashed down
The thunder roared
The lightening illuminated the sky
On that dark, dark night.
It scared me a lot
But I knew that I had to go in it
For I could not stand in the forest of nowhere
In the middle of a thunderstorm.

As I approached it my body trembled,
I asked myself who could possibly live here?
My question was answered as I stepped into the house!
Lots of spiders and at least 50 mice.
I walked up the stairs and into a room
Where I got covered in cobwebs and tripped over a mop.

Then I saw them, a family of ghosts,
As they scattered, I screamed and I cried.
Then I woke up and realised it was all a dream, or was it?
I looked down at my clothes, they were not clean,
They were covered in cobwebs and I had a bruise on my knee.
I don't know whether it was true,
But I do know it could happen to *you!*

Charlene Maher (12)
Loreto Grammar School

I'M A GOLDFISH!

I am small, red and orange,
with white fins and white tail.
I watch you with eyes round and bright,
I'm a goldfish!

My home is a tank
with tasty food and a cave.
Plants and gravel and a lid with a light,
I'm a goldfish!

I swim around with my friends
in water, fresh and so clear
and a thermometer keeping the temperature right,
I'm a goldfish.

I'm a goldfish, I'm a goldfish.
Did I say that before?
Sorry my memory's much better at night,
I'm a goldfish . . . I think!

Karen Finney (12)
Loreto Grammar School

IT'S NOT EASY

Today the teachers told us to write a poem
Everybody's ideas were flowing
But for me it was positively mind-blowing
Whether my poem is funny or sad.

Poems I write, my thoughts are glowing
This list of words is overflowing
I'm in some doubt
I cannot finish, I scream and shout.

Collected thoughts are coming back
Suddenly I'm on the right track
All my words, they fit together
Goodness knows I could go on forever.

So there it is
My hard-thought verse
My brain is swelling
Where's the nurse?

Katie Serridge (13)
Loreto Grammar School

THE HUNKY MONKEY

I'm sitting in the car,
There's just me and my ma,
Ready to go to the zoo.
We arrive at the gates,
When I see all my mates,
So I wave and shout 'Yoo-hoo!'
Then something caught my eye,
To my friends I said, 'Goodbye,'
And I went to see what it was,
It was a brown furry monkey,
Very small, sweet and hunky,
So I decided to show it to my mum.
When my mum saw it,
She had a fit and swore at it,
Then she made me give it back to the zoo.
I gave it to the guy,
To the monkey I said 'Bye,'
Then I screamed and said 'Boo-hoo!'

Julia Price (13)
Loreto Grammar School

BLUE

Blue is a butterfly in the sky,
Blue is a swallow flying by,
Blue is a whale sailing in the sea,
Blue are the jeans that cling to me,
Blue is the ink blob in my book,
And the eyes through which you look,
Blue is a colour of the rainbow that's best,
Blue are the towels we give to our guest.
Blue is my ruler,
Blue is my toy,
Blue is the colour for a baby boy,
I like blue,
Don't you?

Kate Wickstone (13)
Loreto Grammar School

THE THEME PARK

I often go out on days to the theme park,
It all lights up and it's great when it's dark,
Everyone's eating yellow and pink candyfloss,
I didn't go on the ghost train but hey! It's not my loss!
There's this brilliant roller-coaster which I particularly love,
You shoot off really fast and can see everything above.
There's also this water chute that gets you soaking wet,
There's this brilliant new shop where you can buy a cyber pet!
Later on I said, 'We better be going home, my mum might shout.'
So we headed towards the exit and made our own way out.

Victoria Sumner (13)
Loreto Grammar School

THE STORM

Thunder roaring like a monster's cry,
Lightning bolts illuminating the sky.
Trees bending in the gale,
Pelted by both sleet and hail.
Dark clouds rolling in from nowhere,
Weighing down and thickening the air.
Heavy raindrops smash to the ground,
Filling all my sight and sound.
I watch them bouncing off the path
- Mesmerised,
And how they pound the grass
- Hypnotised.
Another flash and eruption of sound
Brings an oak tree crashing down -
A blinding flash of luminous yellow,
Crowning the tree with a burning halo.
The howling wind wails in vain-
The thunder monster's cry of pain.
The trees straining against the monster's breath,
Fear that the storm will bring them to death.
As if in answer to their plea:
For there no rain or wind to be,
The nightmare suddenly subsides -
As if the monster's rage were pacified;
The clouds peel away to reveal the sky,
And no longer can we hear the monster's cry.

Melissa Kidd (13)
Loreto Grammar School

YOU DON'T WANT TO COME TO MY HOUSE

You don't want to come to my house,
There is nothing to eat.
You don't want to come to my house,
You won't get to sleep.

You don't want to come to my house,
There is nothing to play.
You don't want to come to my house,
My sister will drive you away.

You don't want to come to my house,
My dad is so boring.
You don't want to come to my house,
You'll hear my brother snoring.

You don't want to come to my house,
The dog will bite your finger.
You don't want to come to my house,
My mum's a real bad singer.

You don't want to come to my house,
But I'll come to your house,
And be as quiet as a mouse.

Emily Towey (13)
Loreto Grammar School

FIRST DAY AT SCHOOL

Starting school,
I feel such a fool!
I don't think my uniform is very cool.

Late, late get in the gate,
I don't know where I'm going, please wait!
Oh yes! There's my friend Kate.

Sat in the hall feeling down,
Then someone called out my name,
Thank God! I was with Kate again.

Now I think I have no fear,
Now I see all my friends are near,
I think I'm going to like it here!

Lucy Abdulla (11)
Loreto Grammar School

WHEN MY CAT GOT LOST

When my cat got lost it was gone for six hours,
It told me it went everywhere, through bushes, trees and flowers.
She said she was in the garden,
When the next-door neighbour's dog Gordon,
Came running through trying to chase her,
So she ran away, he could have ate her.
She passed the market, all the shops,
She said she ate ten lollipops.

Then she said she went to the park,
That's where she saw her new friend Mark.
He said 'What are you doing here Kitty?'
She said 'Gordon's drunk, he's after me!'
He took her home, Gordon was gone,
Kitty was so happy, she sang a song.

I heard her singing so I ran outside,
I then saw Mark by her side.
I now have two cats Mark and Kitty,
They've just had a baby and called her Mitty.

Katie Lewis (11)
Loreto Grammar School

CHILDHOOD MYTHS

When I was young,
would you believe,
They said the moon
was made of cheese!
But now I know it's just a rock,
and it's not Santa who fills my sock.
And Easter bunnies running riot
laying eggs to ruin my diet.
As for fairies taking teeth,
I'm sorry that's simply beyond belief!
Now and then I wonder why
adults tell children such stupid lies.
Did they never go to school or
are they mad and complete fools?

Suzanne Murray (13)
Loreto Grammar School

FIRST DAY AT SCHOOL

Today's the day, it's here at last,
I'm going to work in a brand new class,
In a brand new building,
In a brand new school,
With brand new teachers,
And their brand new rules.

My hair is tied back neatly,
My shoes are squeaky and clean,
My uniform is neat and tidy,
My blazer hangs down to my knee.

I arrive at school, and say bye, bye to my mum,
And go into my brand new form,
I meet the teacher who has a really weird name,
And I sit at a desk, all thin and plain.

The time goes by, like a fly in the sky,
And the next thing I know,
It's time to go home,
I spot my parents,
Waiting in the car for me,
And go on home, to eat my tea.

Robyn Massey (12)
Loreto Grammar School

MY FIRST DAY AT SCHOOL

I wonder what it's like?
Who am I going to be with?
Where am I going?
Who's that?
The teacher?
I wonder what she's like?
I hope I sit with a friend!
But where are they all?
Where am I?
What am I doing here?
There's nobody around,
What shall I do?
I'll walk through that door.
Everyone is there!
I sit down,
Rest my head on my arm.
I suddenly awake in my bed!
Was that really my first day at school?

Joanne Keys (11)
Loreto Grammar School

AT THE ZOO

Where shall we start?
What shall we see?
Perhaps the monkeys
Swinging in the tree?

Their faces are ugly
Their ears are so big
Their arms are so long
But made to be strong.

Let's move on to the elephants
Big and clompy
Walking around
With their feet so stompy.

Oh look, there's a tiger
Creeping through the grass
Eating a biscuit
No thank you, I'll pass.

Now where are the seals?
Oh look, there they are
Splashing in the water
They can swim so far.

We've been round the zoo
There's nothing to do
But before we go home
We must have finished at the animal zone.

Angela Hardman (11)
Loreto Grammar School

MY BEST FRIEND

Stephanie is my bestest friend,
She never drives me round the bend.
She's different to the rest,
Because she is the best.

She has piercing deep blue eyes,
And her personality is really nice.
Her hair is blondy-brown,
And when I'm around her I never frown.

I hope we can be friends forever,
And never break up never, never.
Stephanie is my bestest friend,
I know she will be till the end.

Helen Tansley (13)
Loreto Grammar School

TIGGER

My cat is a tabby called Tigger,
As cats go you won't find one bigger,
He's incredibly proud, handsome not loud,
And he catches mice with great vigour.
Tigger has fought many battles,
He likes to be king of the street,
But there's many a cat that will challenge that,
But a winner I have yet to meet.

When in a mood he can be quite rude,
And give you swipe with his paw,
But when he is nice, soft, cuddly, and warm,
There's no cat in the world quite like my Tigger.

Sophie Jackson (11)
Loreto Grammar School

KING OF THE WILDERNESS

The wolf stands atop a mountain, stares down below,
Across the magnificent untamed land,
Of a place of eternal snow,
His wilderness kingdom, free from the greed of Man.

Jagged mountains standing tall and proud,
The frozen lake glittering with a bright sheen,
Harsh shrieking storms, and the heavy, grey cloud,
The hungry hunting, pinched and lean.

The white blanket smothering the world with snow,
The wolf's wild howl of the darkest night,
Proclaiming where Man cannot go,
See his silver coat, battered with winter's might.

The ghostly moon hangs in the dark sky,
The predator softly stalking the prey,
The snow owl soaring silently so high,
The nervous rabbits anxiously await the day.

Anna Clarke (12)
Loreto Grammar School

THE MORNING BEFORE SCHOOL

No one was awake but I was,
The sun wasn't up but I was,
No one was dressed but I was,
No one was nervous but I was,
No one was thinking about Loreto but I was,
No one was seeing the visions I had but I was,
No one was praying to God but I was,
      Or maybe they were?

Claire Toland (11)
Loreto Grammar School

MY CAT

Shiny fur
Cold, wet nose
Needle point claws
On the end of her toes.

Green eyes, shining in the night
Morning will find her curled up tight
A warm, black ball
On the foot of my bed
Not a space to be seen
From tail to head.

When the birds awake
She's out through the flap
To let them know the garden belongs
To my cat!

Rachael Murdoch (11)
Loreto Grammar School

HAMMY THE HAMSTER!

A tiny twitcher,
A sharp snapper,
A wheel winder,
A gnawing nibbler,
A comforting crawler,
A furry friend,
A lazy lump,
A bouncing ball,
A mammoth mouth,
A ticking tail.

Sarah Peat (11)
Loreto Grammar School

MARS

As we get ready for take off,
We feel apprehensive, we are the explorers
Of unknown tomorrows.
Our anticipation grows through every zone
Constant travel as our mission goes on, on, on . . .

Discovering new planets and stars,
And naming them as we voyage through,
The dark sky which we call space.
Can we still be called the intelligent life form,
Or is there more?

Suddenly all the orange and yellow hues,
Turn to blues, blacks and purples.
Our pensive moods are reflected by
The newly coloured, murky atmosphere
Our journey ends, with a crescendo as . . .
Starbursts light our way home.

Jessica Robinson (11)
Loreto Grammar School

FIRST DAY AT SCHOOL

I wonder if I'll be with my friends?
I really want this nightmare to end.
School's a breeze,
(or so I thought)
I wish I could remember my 1, 2, 3s.

The tram was late and I've missed my bus
I bet nobody felt as bad as us.
I'm tired, exhausted and ready for bed,
I wish I could get this ache out of my leg.

I'm hungry and I want my tea!
Now I remember how to count to 3!

Oh no! Not another day!
I've forgotten my pass and I'll have to pay.
It's the first day my bus is on time
I can't think of anything to rhyme.

Rachel Clarke (11)
Loreto Grammar School

I AM A FIGMENT OF YOUR IMAGINATION

I am a figment of your imagination.
I have no feelings for you.
I am your creation.
I will lead you in the wrong direction,
Or the one that your brain supposedly tells me to.
I will distort all your thoughts, turn your joy to pain.
Because I, this little figment, have something to gain.

I am a figment of your imagination.
I can run wild.
I can make you think of any man, woman or child.
I am the boss of your heart, brain and soul.
I can make you believe things that are not real.
For I am the one who dictates to you how you really feel.

I am a figment of your imagination.
I can control your whole body.
I can bring feelings of guilt, pangs of anger that won't
Go away until you wilt.
And why do you think I should do all that?
Because you, my friend, are the creator of your own sewer rat!

Jemma Egan (14)
Loreto Grammar School

MOUSE ADVENTURE

In a small old school,
A small brown mouse lives
Scattering on the floor and munching on crisps.
He really didn't care what food he ate
He just munched and munched and said
'Yum this tastes great!'
But have you ever heard of a talking mouse
That chatters all day and talks all night,
The squeals and squeaks and may give you a fright
Well I certainly hadn't
Until the day I heard him say
'Oh, be quiet,' in a funny sort of way,
He once scurried and scratched his paws along
The old wooden floors and swinging his long pink tail
In the air,
He pranced around without a care,
Then the mouse came to a sudden stop,
And hid under the desktop
And as the children came in from play
No one heard the little mouse say,
'I wish I could go back to my hole,
Where I can play with my friend Mole.'
And no sooner had he said it
He was scurrying away
Back to his hole in a quiet sort of way
When he arrived he climbed into bed
Ate some cheese and lay down his little head
And slept for hours until the bell rang
For a start of another day
Of adventures and play!

Fiona McGuire (12)
Loreto Grammar School

MY ONLY PET

My only pet was a dog,
He was as cute as can be,
No one was as loyal to anyone but me.
He ran away from home one day,
And all around the town,
But hard as I could try I couldn't track him down.

We looked all over everywhere,
The park, the shops, the streets,
We even popped into an Allsports shop,
We wouldn't admit defeat.

I hope he comes back home soon,
I miss him quiet a lot,
I wish I'd taken better care of him,
There's pictures all over the shops,
And his favourite place - the park,
I just hope that one day I'll hear again his bark.

Louise Buxton (12)
Loreto Grammar School

THE MASK

Have you ever seen the man behind the face?
The person living the life,
The person drinking the soul.
Have you ever seen him?
Have you ever seen beyond the mask?
We all wear a mask.
Have you ever let anyone through?
He let me through,
The person drinking the soul.
The person living the life.

Katie Davies (14)
Loreto Grammar School

UNDERNEATH THE OCEAN'S SURFACE

Down under the ocean's surface,
Is Neptune and his spooky curses
Wonderful, bright and colourful too,
And don't you wish it could be you.

Sea horses, sharks, turtles and crabs,
But be careful they're not up for grabs.
Whales, fish and many more,
The list could go on forever more.

So don't pollute our oceans
Because pollution makes a large commotion.
Whales and lobsters are dying out,
All because we want to look good when we go out.

Katie Mellett (12)
Loreto Grammar School

A WINTER'S EVENING

The dark draws in on a winter's evening.
The fire's flames are dancing bright.
The sun is setting, the day is leaving.
The trees look eerie in the silvery light.
The sky is black. No, it's dark blue.
For a while it seems so dark,
But now the moon is here with its magical hue.
The hungry fox gives an unsatisfied bark.
The owl sits on a bare frosty bough,
Looking for a poor fieldmouse.
I hope he survives somehow.
I'm glad I am sitting by the warm fire in my house.

Sarah Chester (14)
Loreto Grammar School

FIRST DAY AT SCHOOL

Mum! Mum! Where's my PE kit?
My school uniform doesn't fit!
Where is my bag? Where are my books?
(My mum gives me a dirty look)
Now on my bus I do depart.
My shoes as heavy as my heart.
On my bus are kids, great and small.
Some are short, but most are tall.
But here we are! They let us in!
My goodness what an awful din!
They showed us to our classrooms.
Then we all got out our brand new pens.
And wrote about a big giraffe.
My teacher thought it quite a laugh!
Our bell has rung! Gee oh wow!
Everyone is running now,
To the canteen, we are all in!
Slimy baked beans in a tin!
Smelly cod and chips too,
This is what they give to you!
Lunch is over, back again,
To our nice new classroom.
Then we read and read.
And sit and sit.
Last bell's gone, our eyes are lit!
End of *my* first day, that's it!

Laura Callan (11)
Loreto Grammar School

MY FIRST DAY

I was dripping with sweat,
The playground getting wet.
I looked around . . .
Not a sound,
I'm the only one!
Where's everyone gone?
I walked further in
All that was there
Was a small paper bin
74 was on the door
I quietly knocked
When the door unlocked
There was my friend
Going round the bend
A normal room
Happy . . . no gloom
Then I ran in the door
And said nothing more!

Helen Ward (12)
Loreto Grammar School

THE COW PIG

In the countryside it all started
When the moon shone, shimmering
And the clouds parted
'Look at them, they are lovely,'
Vera said, 'Oh aren't they cuddly?'

We thought it was a cow at first
But its nose was round flat and burst
This little thing was black and white
Its tail was long and in a plait.

It was very podgy and walked rather dodgy
And liked eating flowers and scraps
He sat on my knee and had little naps.

Firm friends we became
Will Thompson was his name
We went everywhere together
And we were buddies forever.

Kate Gaughan (11)
Loreto Grammar School

FRED THE SNAKE

Fred the snake was eight foot three,
He was nearly twice the size of me.
One day in biology in room forty four,
There was a loud knock on the door.
There stood a man from the RSPCA,
Here to give us all a talk today.
'Good morning,' he said, 'I'm called Ted
I'm going to tell you about a snake called Fred.
He's a rather large python, eight foot three in fact
So don't stroke him or touch him to keep your fingers in tact.
So let's all leave Fred just over there
So nobody has any kind of a scare.'
Ted turned his back,
What a mistake,
Ooops, Fred the snake's escaped.

Hayley Smith (13)
Loreto Grammar School

SPRINGY SUE

Now once upon a time, there was a kangaroo,
who was known by the name of Springy Sue.
She was a normal kangaroo up to her hips,
but then came two springs from her waist to toe tips.
Her body was very thin, her eyes big and grey
and her tan coloured fur would sparkle all day.
She was known throughout the world for her unusual legs
and also her collection of doll-faced wooden pegs.
Now strangely one day there came the most terrible blizzard,
so she had to move in with her friend the big lizard.
But there was such a racket made between the lizard and Sue
that she had to move out and go to Peru.
Whilst she was there she met some Guinea-pigs,
but they were nasty and mean so she left in a tick,
but where should she go? What should she do?
So now she moved on to Timbuktu.
Here Sue was happy, for here she looked normal
because all the animals were strange, and never dressed formal.
With her came a cat with two very long tails
and two naughty birds, why I believe they were quails.
'How happy I am,' said Sue to the cat,
'I shall live here forever and forever after that.'

Sarah Hepple (12)
Loreto Grammar School

FIRST DAY AT SCHOOL

I sat in the hall
With a big frown
I really was feeling down
With my uniform too big
And my shoes too small
I really didn't like it at all
I felt so tiny, teachers so big
I had to look up an enormous height
Then the bell rang 1, 2, 3
Everybody went except for me
I was so frightened
I quivered at the knees
Then a teacher came to talk to me
She said 'Relax
Be confident and strong
Then you'll see nothing will go wrong.'
We walked down the corridor arm in arm
It seemed so difficult to stay calm
I walked into the classroom, everybody stared
I felt so lonely, so embarrassed, so scared
Then the bell rang for class to begin
Now I wasn't feeling as dim
We played some games and worked a while
All my fears have disappeared
Now there's no more need for tears.

Jenny Bazill (11)
Loreto Grammar School

FREDRIC

I have a pet tortoise,
A harmless little thing,
He's not at all like a turtle,
Or a terrapin.

My tortoise is a male,
Fredric is his name,
I enjoy being in his company,
He's never ever a pain.

He walks around the garden,
On his own all day,
The only thing he really does,
Is eat and sleep (not play).

I enjoy feeding Fredric,
He enjoys it too,
Fredric enjoys eating lettuce,
But then he needs the loo.

When he goes to the toilet,
He does it on the floor,
I think it's really dirty,
Then he does it even more.

I mean . . .

He doesn't even use toilet paper!
Not at all like me.
My mummy says it's natural,
But we'll just have to see.

Fredric is much older than me,
Twenty-two years to be precise.
For he's now twenty-seven,
And I'm still only five.

I guess when I'm a big girl,
Like my bigger sister Mal,
I'll still have Fredric with me,
'Cause he's my bestest pal.

Emma Divinney (12)
Loreto Grammar School

APPEARANCES

It doesn't matter
What size you are,
Short, fat or thin,
Tall, round or slim.

People shouldn't judge you
By the shape you are,
But rather what's inside you,
And what you have to share.

If you judge people by what
They look like on the outside,
You never get the best
Out of their inside.

And remember, a slim pretty
Person can be spiteful,
Just as a plump, round
Person can be delightful.

Rebecca Swarbrick (14)
Loreto Grammar School

ANGELS OF MERCY

As is sit here in the depths of my self-indulgence,
The sun draws its curtains to the world.
The thunder crashes against the violet sky,
An apocalypse unheard to the world.
The rain has come without warning,
It patters on the roof above my head.
The spiders crawl over the walls,
Hearing my dreams in their heads.

This is the end of the world,
A trickle of blood in the night.
I knew this before you left me:
When you died I lost my soul.

I have lost you as I have lost my will to live,
Knowing you are near yet so far from me.
To see the beauty in each touch:
You touch the world but you cannot touch the pain you feel.

I sense a sorrow in your lonely eyes when you look into mine,
You call to me asking me to join you in your world.
The shadows are hurting you; abusing you,
Testing your power without your one true love.

My tears have already engulfed my heart and now,
You have pronounced the Armageddon of my soul,
As the birds sing their haunted melodies in unison.

Infinite darkness surrounds my heart as a dozen
Angels step out of the shadows,
I know they have come to take me to you.

I have tried to pretend that I have a future,
But my future was denied a long time ago.
I do not deserve this love for I am empty hearted,
When you died you took my heart with your own . . .

Charlotte Burton (14)
Loreto Grammar School

CAT TALK

'Well, what happened to you again?'
Hissed Mitzi, proud and tall.
She sniffed and glared at poor old Ben,
Slumped in a heap on the yard wall.

With whiskers bent and ruffled fur,
Ben looked up and heaved a sigh.
Through reddened eyes he looked at her
With sleek, majestic tail held high.

'That Great Dane from number five,
Barking loud made such a din.
From this high wall, I took a dive
And landed head first in the bin.

Midst wet tea bags and eggshells crushed
I lay bruised and dazed for some long while.
When all around was still and hushed,
I scrambled out and ran a mile.

Home at last! I purred once I'd been fed
And pondered on my recent strife.
Out with the bottles instead of bed,
Now that's what I call a dog's life!'

Beth Westwood (12)
Loreto Grammar School

FIRST DAY AT SCHOOL

I wake up early, starting school today.
Put on my uniform and be on my way.
My mum is crying at the door,
'She's not my baby anymore!'
I get to school right on time
I am okay and I feel fine
We sit on benches talk and say
'I wonder what it'll be like today.'
My name is called out and my friend, Carly's too
I am so nervous I need the loo!
We go to our form rooms and sit at our desks
Mine's got graffiti on it, I think that's grotesque.
We have some lessons and then have a break.
At the tuck shop you can buy cake.
We have some lessons and then Mass,
I think the priest is just plain class.
We have early lunch which is great
I even make a couple more mates
Then finally I go home.
Did you enjoy my rhyming poem?

Vicky Brown (11)
Loreto Grammar School

MY FIRST DAY AT SCHOOL

It's such a big school,
Everything about it is big
The hall, the students, the building,
There are so many people, teachers, and classes.

The school bell goes, once, twice, three times,
People from every corner rush past me
As if they are late for the bus,
Where are they going?
What are they doing?

I turn around a corner, I'm sure room 11 is down there,
Everything goes quiet,
Everything goes dark,
I'm alone in the dark and I'm lost.

Laura McNally (11)
Loreto Grammar School

THE Y FILES

Y does bread land chocolate spread side down?
Y are you only ever ill in the holidays?
Y do you stand for ages waiting for a bus then three come at once?
Y can't pink be for boys and blue be for girls?
Y does your mum always go on the teacher's side?
Y do you never have anything to wear on own clothes day?
Y does your great aunt seem drawn to your cheeks?
Y do your friends go to Turkey and other exotic places and you end up
   in a freezing caravan in Bognor Regis?
Y do you try really hard and still get 'Doesn't try hard enough' on
   your report?
Y do you cry on the day you run out of waterproof mascara?
Y do you not see the boy of your dreams for ages, until you have a bad
   hair day?
Y isn't the world made of chocolate?
Y does your mum always stand nattering for two hours in the freezer
   section of Sainsbury's but doesn't seem to feel the cold?
Y does *he* still not know you're alive?
Y does everything happen in the space of a week?

Eleanor Smith (13)
Loreto Grammar School

MY FIRST DAY AT SCHOOL

At my first day at infant school,
I broke every rule,
In my brand new uniform.

I thought the world would end,
Until I was told I'd make a new friend,
In this strange new school.

I came all prepared,
And older children stared,
As I walked through the door.

I felt really worried until my mum said,
'For goodness sake, you will be fed,'
At this big new school.

At the end of the day I stood at the door to say,
'The day was great, I made a den,
But please don't make me come back again.'

Anne Marie Collins (11)
Loreto Grammar School

FLIGHT OF THE CONCORDE

On a cold October afternoon,
through the cloud so thick and dense,
a large blazing sun peeped through some sky,
and shone on an object whose size was immense.

The object glided on dainty wheels,
Its nose cut through the air,
the tail of the object sparkled at the tip,
and all I could do was gaze and stare.

A shattering noise that this object made,
My ears felt pierced inside and torn,
a hot orange glow fired out of the engine,
and then I realised it was Concorde,

The supersonic rocket strained at first to move,
the wings shook violently,
it then soared high and in a flash,
the Concorde I could no longer see.

Mariann Martinez (14)
Loreto Grammar School

FIRST DAY AT SCHOOL

I sat nervously, waiting to hear who was in my form
When suddenly I saw Cara come,
She looked just like me:
As nervous as can be.
I had my fingers crossed
'I don't know what I'd do without my friends.'
I thought I'd be lost.
'I hope I'm in my friend's class'
I thought as a bunch of sixth formers went past.
The forms were called out
As someone gave a shout.
I looked around and then I found
All my friends gathered around.
'*Yes!* I'm in their class'
I said just as my name was called out last.

Michelle Dooley (11)
Loreto Grammar School

THE SILENT PROWLER . . .

There he walks in the middle of the night,
Trying to be silent with all his might.
While you are all tucked up safe in bed,
He's out hunting and pouncing instead.
Through the grass, gracefully he strides,
In the bushes, quietly he hides.
You might just hear the soft tinkling of the bell,
He has on his collar, but he keeps quiet quite well.
Along the rooftops he silently walks,
Listening for sounds especially bird squawks.
When he sees a bird, a blue tit maybe,
He'll get ready to pounce so silently.
So when you're in bed, and everyone sleeps,
Just think of the Shadow Cat, while silently he creeps.

Lauren Catherine Eley (11)
Loreto Grammar School

FIRST DAY AT SCHOOL

The school bell rings, your heart has stopped
Oh I wish I had chickenpox
So I could stay at home and not come to school,
With all of these people and all of these rooms.

As you walk through the doors I swear you must shrink
For everyone's taller or so you may think,
A teacher comes in, you have to stand up!
Then she hands out a load of exercise books.

At the end of the day the school bell rings,
So I pack up my books and all of my things
Then I walk home, with a smile on my face
To tell my mum everything that happened today.

Sasha Fasolilli (11)
Loreto Grammar School

MY FIRST DAY AT SCHOOL

Breakfast is over,
My lift is here,
Butterflies in tummy,
I'm full of fear,
Books and kit,
My bag is full,
I'm so excited,
But the weather is dull,
All new people, all new faces
Lots of teachers
With briefcases.
I know I'll be busy,
With lots of work,
But it looks interesting,
So I won't shirk,
The biggest playground,
I ever did see,
Was before my eyes,
How lucky I would be.
Different people
Big and small,
Different sizes,
Short and tall,
Now I'm here too,
To do my best,
I'm going to work hard,
With lots of zest.

Rachel Gallagher (11)
Loreto Grammar School

MY WINDOW

The vast expanse of nothingness, embedded with stars aglow,
The swirling evening mist forms clouds outside my window.
The tree at the foot of our garden sways lightly in the breeze,
Everything is quiet and the world, for a change, is at ease.

I stand here and gaze through my window, alone in the darkened room,
Watching the cats on the garden fence, the sky full of sadness
                                                    and gloom.
My reflection glares back from my window, anxiously staring at me,
One million questions are passed in my mind, refusing to let me be.

Gazing up at the dazzling full moon,
Memories flood back, too soon, too soon.
They aren't mine, but someone else's to buy,
A thousand unwanted images, haunting me, refusing to die.

They are images of war, sadness and pain,
Images of corruption, fighting insane.
Shuddering at the thought of such a past,
I stepped back from my window and the sky so vast.

The images have vanished now, all that's left are the stars,
Twinkling so brightly around Jupiter and Mars.
A million sparkling jewels in a dark velvet backdrop,
A million stories to be told at each starry stop.

But as I gaze up, there's one solitary star set apart from the rest,
Shooting across the studded sky in a fiery chariot,
A lone ranger on some mission - some unknown guest.

It's racing across the sky now, like a rocket, sling-shotted into the air,
Travelling with such energy, mapping a course where no one dare.
The little star shoots through the terrestrial sky, full of life and mirth,
Oblivious to all the heartache and pain below it on planet Earth.

Stepping away from my window now, my watch reads half past twelve,
I'll climb into bed with a wondering head,
And in search of the truth, into sleep I'll delve.

Emma Jayne Chebrika (14)
Loreto Grammar School

LOVE!

'Love is blind,'
That's what they say,
Those parents who
Are old and grey.

'You can't see past,
Those deep blue eyes,
Past his dimples,
Or his lies.'

'For all you know,
He could be in crime,
Doing drugs,
From time to time.'

My mum she has told me,
Two million times,
'Be careful,
He's probably buying time.'

Oh, I do wish,
That she could see,
What he's like,
When he's alone with me.

Stephanie Crosbie (14)
Loreto Grammar School

THE TEACHERS

Here's the gang of teachers,
From Loreto Grammar School,
They're very fussy creatures,
But they've broken every rule.

One has a pink moustache,
And badly dyed green hair,
She's always late for lessons,
And wears droopy underwear!

The music teacher is,
A really crazy thing,
She stands on the piano,
And then begins to sing!

The PE teacher thinks she's fit,
But I know that she's not,
I saw her eat ten cream cakes,
Before she putt the shot!

In science there's a reaction,
When teacher enters the room,
There's a fizz, a bang, a crash,
And then a big, big *boom!*

The history teacher's sixteen,
She hasn't a degree,
Her idea of ancient history,
Is 1963 (The Beatles).

As you can see quite clearly,
They're all stark raving mad,
But look at all us children,
What real chance have they had?

Catherine Reed (14)
Loreto Grammar School

THE ACCIDENT

From the moment you were born,
I tried to protect you,
Surrounded by my love,
no one could ever hurt you.
Your soft face against my harsh skin,
so innocent, and sweet.
It's hard to believe what hell we could meet.
I love you.

It was your first day at school,
I was so proud. In your new uniform,
with that smile on your face.
You looked like my angel,
a dream that came true.
If only your daddy could see you too. I love you.

I remember the day when you went out to play,
'Be back by lunch,' I remember shouting,
If only I had known,
I could have stopped you.
The police came knocking at my door.
Your son has been in an accident, a hit and run.
I am sorry son. I love you.

Standing by your bed, still no movement.
All the memories, all the sadness.
Is that a flicker? No.
Yes, he is opening his eyes.
'Hi, Mum, what happened?'
'You have been in an accident.'
'Cool, can we go home?'
'Yes son.'
I love you.

Anita McGuckin (14)
Loreto Grammar School

STARS

Through the peaceful vales I peek,
To catch a glimpse of the shimmering sky,
Up above the conquering lanterns,
Stars twinkle to the dreaming race below.

One star glistens on its own,
Waiting for the night to end,
And for his companions to reveal their splendour.

They guide the strayed,
Give light to the sightless,
And help the lonely to feel cherished.

The shooting star glides through the sky,
Peacefully and calmly,
Waking no one.

As the moonlight begins to fade,
And the stars return to their dwelling,
I sit back and watch the sunlight
Dawn into another day.

Laura McGeagh (14)
Loreto Grammar School

MY LOVE FOR YOU IS GROWING

My love for you is growing,
More and more each day,
And every time I see you,
You take my breath away.
I think about you all the time,
Your name is a constant ringing chime.

I really, really like you,
As I am sure you can tell,
I just have to express how I feel,
This is the best way I can tell.
I think you are fantastic, perfect in every way,
I really, really love you, that's simply all that I can say.

Nicola Young (14)
Loreto Grammar School

SEASUCH

This beautiful place called Seasuch,
Has sandy beaches, soft to touch.
Blue waters that shimmer in the sun,
And trees that blow in the winter breeze.

Seagulls and guillemots fill the sky,
Floating about all over the surf.
While crabs and jellyfish rule the land,
With shells and mussels lying on the sand.

This was before the disaster struck,
When this haven was invaded by people,
Who cared not for the beauty of Seasuch,
And then left it for others to touch.

Cans, bottles and dead birds floated on brown sludge,
When the ghastly oil tank burst to smithereens,
And rescue boats came dashing out,
To save the choking birds.

Underfoot grows no more grass,
Black and dead, this forest that I pass,
Only the polluted air left on which to gasp,
And the traffic hurtling past.

Catherine Broadbent (14)
Loreto Grammar School

MY ANNOYING SISTER

My sister is so very annoying,
I remember once when it was snowing,
She put a snowball down my back,
And then gave it a good, hard whack!

Another thing that's really bad,
Was when she made me feel mad.
When I was fast asleep in bed,
She wrote *'Hit me'* on my head.

There was this time when I was ill,
My mum told her to fetch a pill.
Instead of this she lifted her toes,
And then stuck them right up my nose.

Three years ago, on Hallowe'en
She did something so very mean.
As little kids were passing by,
She jumped out on them and made some cry.

We went to Devon for a holiday,
It was good fun, I really must say,
Apart from one time when I got in a biff
'Cause she tried to push me off the edge of a cliff.

Oh well, I think I'll have to go,
I've got some yelling to do, you know.
She's not tidied up our room you see,
And she's always putting the blame on me.

Angela Johnson (14)
Loreto Grammar School

INDIVIDUALITY

Is it possible?
Could it be?
Is it safe? - No, no!
There it is again,
The barricade of life,
Society's prejudices,
Life's injustices.
When is it my turn?

I'm not allowed to be.
I'm like a bird in a cage.
Helpless in a world of machines,
A person in a robot.
Security, freedom,
There for the taking,
But not for me!
Emotions struggling,
Needs yearning,
When is it my turn?

Trapped by fear,
Consumed by normality,
A need to be,
A right to live,
A wish to love.
When is it my turn?

Zara Longlands (16)
Loreto Grammar School

I Wish . . .

I wish I was older,
I would have much more fun.
I could drive anywhere,
To the moon, to the sun.

I could live on my own,
Or with friends in a flat
And go out every night,
Have a boyfriend called Matt.

I wish I was younger,
At primary school,
Every Monday morning
At the swimming pool.

I wouldn't have to work
Doing jobs round the house,
I could play in the garden,
Look after my mouse.

I wish I was a mum,
So I could have a baby,
I would go to the park
And the zoo - maybe.

And when she grows up,
I'd be by her side,
I'll go to her wedding,
And be full of pride.

After all that I've said,
I'm proud to be me.
I have many friends,
And I love my family.

I go out a lot,
No matter what I say.
I just wish my daughter
Will say the same, one day.

Sophie Chinnery (14)
Loreto Grammar School

THE GLORIES OF WAR

All alone in the darkness of the night,
I have nowhere to turn; I've lost the fight.
Hunched in the corner of a lifeless room,
I see smoke rising amid the silver moon.
Whimpers and screams echo through the harrowing night,
They come from men who are too tired to fight.
Tears are streaming down my cut and bruised face,
I hobble and stumble in hope of getting to my base.
My friends are dead and the enemy is near,
I try to console myself but I am filled with fear.
The *bangs* and *booms* are becoming shorter,
My thoughts are concentrated on my wife and daughter.
My family are safe, tucked up in their beds,
While happy and gentle dreams drift through their heads.
When I came to fight, I was as strong as cement,
But now I am weak, hungry and bent.
I was told war was a man's job, a chance of being a hero,
But I am reduced to nothing, a loser, a zero.

Hayley Campbell (14)
Loreto Grammar School

MY BEST FRIEND

Every morning bright and early, Dad and I go down the lane,
Standing by the fence and waiting, Ted is there with his friend, Shane.

When they see the car approaching, Shane who's always very shy,
Runs along the hedge and hides, we laugh and say we don't know why.

Ted stays there in all his glory, nostrils flared and tail held high,
Prancing on all fours impatient, knowing that a treat is nigh.

He nuzzles into my palm softly, sniffing for his favourite snack,
Polos, mint cake, apples, crusties, then tack up for a hack.

Ted's quite old now, eight and twenty, but his heart is young and gay,
In his eye is still the twinkle, of times gone by in barns of hay.

His smooth brown coat still clean and shiny, his mane still long
                                                        and tangle free.
Muscles still so firm and rippling and that's all down to Ted . . . and me.

Exercise is the secret, teamed with time and constant dare,
Long hot summers, short cold winters, but mostly tender loving care.

We have been together for so long and I know he will do me no wrong,
We will go on till the end, cos Ted will always be my best friend.

Colleen O'Connor (14)
Loreto Grammar School

RAID

The clashing hooves against the mud and stones,
Cheerful laughter followed by endless groans.
The festival banners replaced by a burning town,
Hysteria, chaos and misery all around.
A thunderous order sounding from a man on a horse,
Who's letting this evil run its terrible course.

The smell of *death* lingering everywhere,
But all I could do was stand and stare.
The gallops behind me and the man up ahead,
With his lethal cross and bow aimed right at my head.
My body was frozen; my feet *stuck* to the ground,
My brain told me *move,* but I could not turn round.
I was beginning to wish that I wasn't so sober,
I had no time to dwell, because then it was over.

Jennifer Dunne (14)
Loreto Grammar School

LABORATORY ANIMALS

I was taken from my mother at a very young age,
And thrown in a tiny, wrought iron cage.
I had such hopes and dreams for my life,
Even to be patted more than just twice.
I stood barking excitedly at the bars,
Waiting for someone to come and make me theirs.
Then along came a man wearing a white coat,
And stuck a sharp needle into my throat.
My mind went all dizzy,
I started to shake,
I thought how much more of this can I take?
As the days went on, all the other dogs had gone,
And their cages stood empty and dark.
I didn't have any energy to fight off the men,
Anyway it was pointless to bark.
Then one day as the needle went in,
The pain was sharper than ever.
There was nothing left to do,
My heart had stopped,
Just so that you could have better shampoo.

Sian Scaife (14)
Loreto Grammar School

ONE MISTY MORNING

One misty morning,
I walked out to see,
What but a pussy cat,
Waiting outside for me.

His eyes stared probingly
From his perch in the tree.
He glared down suspiciously
Straight at me.

I strolled past airily,
While his nose twitched warily.
He sniffed the air and raised his paw
And then jumped down to the floor.

He cocked his head with teeming pride
And then bounced playfully to my side.
He began to rub around my legs,
Round and round as if to beg,
For my hand to move his way,
And stroke him from head to tail, all day.

He purred and purred and purred again,
While we wandered past the den.
Then when we had reached the stream,
He flopped to one side and began to dream.

Victoria Montgomery (14)
Loreto Grammar School

TRAFFIC JAM!

One in front,
One behind,
One to the side,
Many cars whizzing through my mind.

So many cars,
Such a little space,
So many people,
Such a short amount of time.

Where is everybody going?
Why all at the same time?
So much impatience,
Faces of frustration.

Got to get home,
Got to cook the tea,
Got to tidy up,
Why can't they see?

Surely if we just got going,
It would be over soon?
They don't have to race,
If they just calmed down surely we would
get home at a much faster pace?

No solutions to the problem,
Who invented it?
What a thing to do,
The traffic jam - such a waste of time!

Fiona McGrory (14)
Loreto Grammar School

FRIENDS TILL THE END!

Soldier, soldier,
You're at war,
You may think it's nothing more,
You may think it's just a game,
But soon you'll never think the same,
Once the guns are fun no more,
I hope you've learnt the law of war.

Soldier, soldier,
You're my friend,
Please don't break or even bend,
If the pressure is too much,
Reach out for a friendly touch,
As your friends will always be,
By your side or guiding thee.

You may experience some awful things,
Or even some unlawful beings,
Even though you'll always know,
You'll have your friends through high or low,
Your friends will be with you all the way,
Yesterday, tomorrow, or even today,
So just remember when you are sad,
We'll be with you through the good and bad.

Joanne McIvor (14)
Loreto Grammar School

THE RED SKY

Forget all that this very moment conveys.
Throw open your windows,
Free the fiery smoke of your dreams.
Look out over the city.

Red sky to tell untold tales of ours.

To all hearts wary,
For all who hate
Tomorrow's days and hours,
Join me.
Dwell with the red sky of
All our yesterdays.

Margaret Barry (16)
Loreto Grammar School

THE SUN GOD

Her power is endless
As she sweeps her warmth across a path of infinity.
If things come too close, she will devour them mercilessly,
Letting out her slick, snaking tongues
And severing them with the lick of death.
Hail the sun!
Her locks flow out into the Earth's atmosphere
Her robe cascades over us all
She sits contented on her majestic, incandescent throne
And eyes the Earth: her glorious empire.
Hail the sun!
She has little rest: only the night,
When her sons and daughters take over: the stars,
But they are merely weak candlelights
And their beams put together are only an infinitesimal fraction of hers.

Hail the sun!
One day she will expire,
Her youthful waves will extinguish into shadowy, sombre darkness.
Her white eyelids will lock into place
And Earth shall be no more.

Isabelle Duck (15)
Loreto Grammar School

INSOMNIAC'S NIGHTMARE

It's now two o'clock, and I'm here in my bed,
A million strange thoughts whizz through my head,
Anyone normal would be sleeping so deep,
But 10 million noises prevent me from sleep.
The hum of a TV somewhere downstairs,
a cat is yowling, quite unaware,
that the dog next door is ready to harm.
plus the continual beeping of a nearby car alarm.
The tap in the bathroom annoyingly drops,
and a noisy gang outside my house stops.
It's now half past two and I'm still awake,
The tap is still dripping,
the cat is still yowling,
the dog is still growling.
Downstairs the TV is switched on so loud
Outside my house is a rowdy young crowd.
All of these noises spin around in my head
Oh, what is the point of lying in bed?
If you can't get to sleep, nor want to get up
when the world and his wife don't know how to
Shut up!
'Don't shout so loud, it's a quarter to three!'
The neighbours are shouting directly at me.
But all I can do is sit here and stare,
another sleepless night, an insomniac's nightmare.

Michelle Farrington (14)
Loreto Grammar School

THE BEACH

The waves lapped gently,
Trying to resist the horizon's pull,
The sand swirled round and round
And the sun shone bright and full.

No people could be seen
When from east to west I scanned.
Everything was still,
Except the dancing of the sand.

I sat high on the cliff top,
Surveying the beauty below,
The tiny glistening rock pools,
And the seaweed's shiny glow.

All was calm, I was alone.

Then I heard the first sounds
And knew my solitude would be broken.
The campers and the tourists,
Like me, had just awoken.

Families began to invade the beach,
Screaming children everywhere.
Noisy games and shouts of swimmers
Filled the early morning air.

Then more and more people came,
And I left my peaceful spot.
I knew the beach would keep filling up
As the sun was nice and hot.

All was chaos, I decided to leave for home.

Catherine Burgis (14)
Loreto Grammar School

WHAT IF . . . ?

They stand there in their groups,
Kicking a football around,
Throwing a pebble up in the air,
Or tackling a defender to the ground.

The subject of this thought, you see,
Is something very puzzling to me,
I'd love to know the life of boys,
And what goes on amidst the noise.

What do they talk about when we're not around?
Why do they write with sticks in the ground?
Why do they go silent when we approach?
Why do they always make noise on a coach?

Oh well, the school bell rings again,
We all file by in groups of ten.
And still I wonder what goes on,
When all is still and when we're gone.

I know my wish will never come,
And so, I will not ask my mum,
To change my first name into Biff,
Though just for one day would be nice; what if . . . ?

Helen Waldron (14)
Loreto Grammar School

WHERE WERE YOU

Where were you when I was born,
When I took my first step, said my first word?
They were the things you never saw or heard.

You never realised how much you hurt me,
My life wasn't complete without you by my side.
For all the times I wanted you, you would run and hide.

Now I'm growing up and trying to fend on my own,
And you still won't and can't care.
I'd challenge you to love me, but you wouldn't dare.

Lyndsey Oughton (14)
Loreto Grammar School

FREEDOM

The window opened setting her free.
She lifted her arms high above her head and broke away.
She was outside now and could feel the wind gently touch her face.
Her hair glistened in the sun as she flew higher in the sky.
The stress of the city faded away.
She was alone with her thoughts.
Alone in the blue sky which seemed not to end.
The clouds delicately floated past her.
She was like them now, aimlessly flying around without a care
in the world.
The palm trees shimmered in the wind.
The sea sparkled like a gigantic pot of glitter.
She floated a bit above the sea.
She could see her reflection in it.
She stretched her arms out and touched the water, making ripples.
She could see the fish swimming in the sun like rays of light shining
through a crack in a dark cave.
The water calmly crashed against the rocks.
She weaved her way through tangled roots of old trees.
She swooped and dived through the air.
She could do what she wanted now, she was free.

Caitriona McLaughlin (14)
Loreto Grammar School

AFTERGLOW

Darkness binds the threads of night
That mark the path of light's retreat,
That pull the lace from on your eyes
To leave sight dark with a crimson hue.

No silence dwells amongst the dim
But quiet suffocates around
Wrapping your head with noiselessness
And filling your ears with the nothing sound.

Draw the shadows close
About the whispers of the night
And let your spirit softly fly
Through the dark.

Anna Scaife (17)
Loreto Grammar School

DON'T YOU LOVE THE RAIN?

Don't you love the rain?
Sounding like drawing pins of glass falling on a tile floor,
A swirling whirling shower of heaven,
Don't you love the rain?
It dribbles into your eyes and drips over your chin,
Into the freshness of a newly cleaned world,
Don't you love the rain?
The fragile clarity that reflects the innermost soul,
A dripping, slipping awash on the windowpane,
How can't you love the rain?

Tracy Rees (18)
Loreto Grammar School

MUMMY'S ANGELS

A kaleidoscope of beautiful colours,
reflect off the sparkling crisp white snow,
onto her pale yellow face.
A set of tiny footprints
sank into the white snow;
next to hers.
A small, warm, living hand,
was placed through her dying one,
like a help to go on.
She felt that she was drowning,
in a sea of sorrow and pain
wanting to take her last gasp,
before being whisked to the surface,
and up far away,
taken by God's angels to an everlasting world,
where her pain is not possible.
The small child at her cold hand.
leapt gaily up and down,
for he knew not that angels
would soon take his dear mummy.
Only the angels and she
knew that little secret.
Soon, her beloved son would be left,
his mother gone to an eternal rest,
to grow without a mother's love, care and devotion.
She knelt beside him in the freezing snow,
and embraced him softly
and she whispered into his cold, red ear:
'I love you'
He smiled, and then Mummy's angels came . . .

Lisa Callaghan (14)
Loreto Grammar School

THE BABBLING BROOK

Sitting by a babbling brook,
Suddenly a picture took,
I watched its journey across the stones,
Twisting and turning as it roams.

The trees gathered as if to listen,
To the babbling brook,
Froth and glisten,
And the grass did whisper,
To the trees,
Whose message was carried in the breeze.

The image formed for all to see,
No more clear than it was for me,
A reflection of my spirit running free,
I knew that my life belonged to me.

Amanda Collier (15)
Loreto Grammar School

THANK YOU

Thank you for looking after me throughout the years,
For making me smile when I've got tears,
I've known you since I was five years old,
From when I was naughty and had to be told,
The loving you give; the patience you have,
The fun you've got has always made me laugh,
You've fed me with sweets and crisps galore,
So much I never had to ask for more,
I'll never forget what a great person you are,
I'll try to visit 'cause you're not very far,
Thank you again for being so kind,
I will never forget you.

Leanne Paton (14)
Loreto Grammar School

I Cannot Believe That She Is Gone

I opened my mouth, but nothing came out,
As hard as I tried, no words could I utter.
I stood, cold and empty,
I could not believe, that she was gone.

I felt numb, I could not move,
When I fell she could not comfort me,
I could not laugh or joke with her,
I could not believe, that she had gone.

I stand all alone now, in my empty world.
There is no one to hug me when I am sad,
There is no one to enjoy my life with me,
I cannot believe that she is gone.

Alicia Cassidy (14)
Loreto Grammar School

Without You

I have no feeling, nothing inside.
There is no solitude where I can hide,
I can't be alone, not even to cry,
My tears inside will never run dry.

You gave me joy and laughter too,
There are parts of me, that are also you,
Now you're gone it's very clear,
My life isn't complete without you here.

Anne Lomas (14)
Loreto Grammar School

LIFE

My life seems to be withering away,
Year after month after week after day,
Fourteen January the firsts, birthdays and Easters,
Fourteen times Santa has come to greet us.

Life is all about being busy,
Waking up in the morning and getting ready,
Getting to the place you know best,
By bus, by train, by car but certainly fast.

Now you're there be it school work or play,
And that is where you spend the rest of your day,
Apart from the hour in the middle of the chaos,
Where you eat your sandwiches and drink from your thermos.

The day is over and you're on your way home,
Getting the tea on and giving the dog its bone,
Before you know it is time for bed,
A few hours sleep and then you're doing it all again.

Lucy Fox (14)
Loreto Grammar School

MOVING FAR AWAY

They didn't realise how it would change her,
They didn't seem to care how she felt.
Nobody asked what her opinion was,
It was going to happen and that was that.

They didn't understand what she had to leave,
They didn't consider what the other options were.
Nobody stopped to think how upset she would be,
Or realise the pain she would suffer.

And what would she do now she was all alone,
So far away with no one to turn to.
All she could do was frown and cry herself to sleep,
All she could do was plan to run away to back where she belonged.

Catherine Adamson (14)
Loreto Grammar School

SHE

All she ever wanted was to be loved,
Loved like all the others,
Was that too much to ask
From her mother and sister and brothers?

She craved all the attention she'd never had
Attention she was entitled to.
She didn't understand how to get it,
She didn't know what to do.

She felt like a stranger among those she knew,
A stranger who was intruding,
She wanted to belong there
She didn't want to be the one they were excluding.

If she left, no one would notice,
Or at least, they wouldn't care,
How long before they'd come looking
When they realised she wasn't there?

But none of that matters anymore.
The thoughts are no longer in her head
As she lies back and looks up
Out of her earthy bed.

Rachel Daly (18)
Loreto Grammar School

THE DREAM I HAD LAST NIGHT

The buzz of the alarm
Breaks the calm
Of the dream I had last night.
Go away morning
Don't remind me of the boring
Day I have ahead.
I dreamt I was flying
And the birds were trying
To fly higher than me;
But they couldn't.
The clouds were like pillows
And looked like the smoke
That billowed from down below.
They tasted like candyfloss
That had been spun and tossed
By angels with little white wings.
I carried on through
The beautiful blue
Horizon I had ahead.
I flew low
I flew high
Through the silent blue sky
Watching the people like ants below.
The dream was great
Until I woke up with hate
Of the alarm that bleeped so loud.
I wanted to go back
With the dream still intact
But I couldn't get back to sleep.
I suppose it's all right
As there's always tonight
To dream of whatever I want.

Natalie Cowan Heath (14)
Loreto Grammar School

MY SHADOW

Following behind me,
Nowhere else to go,
Silently chasing,
It's my friend the shadow.

I think she must like me,
She never leaves my side,
If she's not in front of me,
I turn and she's behind.

Sometimes she's big,
Sometimes she's small,
And if I wake up early
She's not there at all.

She doesn't seem to do a lot,
She has no life of her own,
She has no facial features
And makes no moans or groans.

I wonder what her name is
If she has one at all?
If only we could communicate
I'm sure we'd have a ball!

I wonder if she'll be with me forever
And will our friendship grow?
I'm glad I never feel alone
With my friend the shadow.

Jennifer Hopewell (14)
Loreto Grammar School

THE FIRST DAY

My first day of school, I couldn't believe it,
I was all ready with my bag and PE kit.
I stood in the playground waiting for the bell,
Wondering which teacher was mine, I could not tell.

As it turned out my teacher was Mrs Pew,
She seemed quite nice as far as I knew.
Our classroom was not what I had expected,
It looked a bit like it had been neglected.

All morning we sang,
Until the bell rang.
We went to the playground for the second time that day,
Where all of the children had begun to play.

That afternoon we did colouring in,
And we stuck mine on the wall, with my name, Daniel Kin.
Then the bell rang for us all to go home,
And off I went underneath our hall dome.

Overall I would say the day was a success,
My first day of school in the school of Little Loch Ness.

Rebecca Garvey (14)
Loreto Grammar School

MY WORLD

I live in a world so empty and cold,
No one to have, no one to hold.
I dream of love so happy and true,
As happy as I was when I was with you.

I dream of a world full of love,
A world of peace represented by a dove.
All the wars and fighting will end,
And the world will live in peace as friends.

All the world will love and care,
Be as one, learn to share.
Every day will be filled with joy,
Filled with the laughter of every girl and boy.

Genevieve Reynolds (14)
Loreto Grammar School

THE SENILE CREATURE

His skin is wrinkled like a crumpled tissue
As his eyes gaze from under sagging bags.
His colouring is pale as though frost has passed
And kissed his delicate skin.
The position of his teeth is random like pegs in a classroom
As they peak out from his pleated curtained lips.

His back is arched like a scythe on a spring day
Which creaks painfully as each step is taken.
His bent fingers resemble hooks grasping his
only companion; his walking stick.
The ball-legged feet give him little support these days
Making him amble ridiculously, his feet barely leaving the ground.

As I watch this old man whilst passing by,
I smile kindly out of sympathy.
He smiles back and in his sparkling button eyes,
I see the forgotten youth of a lost child.
Thinking what is to happen in my coming years,
I keep my memory of a wonderful senile creature.

Julia Krysiak (14)
Loreto Grammar School

WILL YOU LEND ME SOME MONEY?

Dad, will you lend me some money today?
No my dear honey, as I have not much money,
Now run along my dear, go and play.

Dad, will you lend me some money? I'm desperate, I am.
No, no, my dear little lamb,
Because the dog's got my wallet,
He just sort of swallowed it,
Now, I'll give you some another day, if I can.

Dad, can I have some money right now?
Now, my darling, don't start a row,
I don't like your tone of voice with me
and while you're here, don't you see,
I have no money the choice is no other,
I tell you what, go and ask your mother.

Dad, I've been thinking about what you've said to me,
The other day I found the key to the safe,
in the office by the chair, you see?
I opened it wide and to my surprise
a stash full of money, you've been telling me lies.

So dad, I've come to this conclusion right here,
Come now, let's get these facts clear,
It's not the fact that you can't or don't,
The fact remains the simplest, my dear,
It's simply the fact that you won't.

Chloé Taberner (14)
Loreto Grammar School

THE EMPTY PAGE

The stark vastness of the page staring me in the face,
'The whole page to be filled, not a spot of white,'
Mrs Potts' voice clear in my ear,
Oh where to start, how to fill it!

Then the colours - red, blue, yellow,
orange, purple and black.
So many from which to choose.
Oh where to start, how to fill it!

A picture to copy, picked randomly for me.
'Think very seriously - tone and texture,'
Mrs Potts' voice clear in my ear,
Oh where to start, how to fill it!

'Make a start - now don't be scared.
Just observe and record what you see,'
Mrs Potts' voice clear in my ear,
Oh where to start, how to fill it!

A hive of activity, all but me!
Paint wash or detail - which is it to be?
Burning sensation all down my arm,
Mrs Potts' coffee all over me.

In the sick bay. Back to square one -
The stark vastness of the walls staring me in the face . . .

Laura Hunter (14)
Loreto Grammar School

THE GIRL WHO NEVER GETS PICKED!

If you look on the games field closely,
If you watch the girls in PE,
You will see all the runners and jumpers,
And on the touchline, you'll see me.

For I am the last in the races,
The one who always gets licked,
The person who's not so brilliant,
I'm the girl who never gets picked.

I can't get the hang of the high jump,
While others do it with ease,
I never get chosen for netball,
I stand on the touchline and freeze.

Once when Sarah was missing,
I was called from the sidelines to play.
But, the others wouldn't pass me the ball,
And shouted 'Where's Sarah today?'

At my school we don't have aerobics,
We have hockey, netball and running.
Life is just one competition
And my lack of aggression is stunning.

On sports day we've long jump and shot-put
And thousands of ways to get fitter.
But nothing for my disposition
Except helping to collect all the litter!

Clare Mary Seccombe (14)
Loreto Grammar School

THE GUILT RUNS DEEP

Blood saturates the shambolic land,
Made suppurative by the unnatural forces
Of Man's uncontrollable fury,
As we abandon again our finer feelings
Of compassion, clemency and control.
Are any of us innocent?

It's probably happening today, in
Chechnya, or El Salvador, or The Golan Heights,
Northern Ireland, or Kosovo, or Thailand, or Uganda -
Whole countries forced into wars,
They do not want or do not need,
But it is the innocent who suffer.

The leaders of the world justify their actions.
They exclaim, they have learnt their lesson
From previous war; but suddenly murder is acceptable.
The gun solves their perennial problems,
No one will listen or negotiate anymore,
They have lost their innocence.

Politicians have people sacrificed
For their own egos; in the name of religion,
Race, or merely a good idea.
Their decisions decimate mankind.
I am not looking for an ideal world,
I am just sick with the bloodshed in this one.
I want to remain innocent.

Josephine Eccles (14)
Loreto Grammar School

THE PHONE CALL

Here I sit, waiting . . . waiting for what?
Perhaps a message from a friend,
or maybe a foe?
It's simply a case of waiting because I just don't know.

There's nothing to do,
So I just sit, reading the paper,
Occasionally, looking out of the window, glancing,
I see raindrops dancing.

It's now five past eight
and getting very late.
I can't help but groan,
as I'm waiting for my love to phone.

I long for the phone to ring.
It's been over an hour
and the rain is now a shower.
So I've given up all hope,
I will retreat to my bedroom,
There I can mope and hide my gloom.
But wait . . .
What is that I hear?
Ringing right through my ear.
I think it's the phone,
now I hear the dulcet tone.
I pick up the receiver, having a feeling it's her.
Now I can rest assured,
that my love has called.

Siobhan Guilfoyle (14)
Loreto Grammar School

BULLY

Bully, bully go away from me
Bully, bully stop hitting me
Bully, bully why do you do it?
Bully, bully your friends are driving you to it
Bully, bully you are sad
Bully, bully you make me mad
Bully, bully you bully too much
Bully, bully why do you touch?

Leian White (14)
Manor High School

THE BLACK FOX

Silently, slowly without a sound,
A coal-black fox appears from the ground.
Her golden eyes search the woods,
A wet, pointed snout smells something good.
Her white-tipped tail as light as a plume,
Flows behind her as she races into the gloom.
Over the rocks as easily as a cat,
She runs and pounces upon a rat.
Joyfully she turns right round
And silently heads back towards the den in the ground.
She feels no sadness that the rat is dead,
Because now her young cub is soon to be fed.
Silently, quickly without a sound,
A coal-black fox disappears back into the ground.

Jennie King (12)
New Wellington School

THE BLACK FOX

It was one dark night
When I watched him take flight
And speed into some trees
His tail was long and bushy
And his fur rippled in the breeze
I glimpsed his pointed face
His beady eyes alert
As if he was saying 'I'm a tiny fox
And I'm scared of getting hurt'
I must run now to find some food like anyone, to stay alive
But the men with guns in the darkened woods
Don't want us to survive
They think it's fun to see us run
And watch us die in pain
I'm a cunning fox, and I run so well
But I don't like to play this game
I want to be in my foxes' den, with my family safe and sound
I don't want to hear the deafening guns and thud of great big hounds.

Ben Morris (11)
New Wellington School

BONFIRE NIGHT

Bonfire Night is great.
All of the fireworks light up the sky, some are low,
some are high, some bang, some fizz, some stay on the ground,
some go high up in the sky.
I love watching the fireworks from my bedroom window,
and all the children playing, but the one thing I hate worst of all
is all of the deaths that have come from Bonfire Night.
I love Bonfire Night, it is great.

Kimberley Latham (11)
New Wellington School

THE BLACK FOX

Over the rocks and through the trees,
Under the bush with such great ease.
Her movements are quick and always flow,
Taking her where she wants to go.
Her ears up high just like a sail,
I could see the white tip at the end of her tail.
Her black legs shining in the sun,
This fox is quick, she knows how to run.
She looked at me with golden eyes,
Gave a bark and to my surprise,
Out came a cub with a stubby nose,
Ears curled up like a little rose.
Its eyes are brown unlike its mother,
I wonder are there any others?

Gemma Chapman (11)
New Wellington School

THE BLACK FOX

Foxes can be slick,
They are so quick,
When it comes to food,
They can be so rude,
They root in bins
and scrounge for things.

At night they come alight,
They hunt for voles,
Which live in holes
and her fur is the colour
of coal.

Gemma Hancox (11)
New Wellington School

THE AUTHOR OF THIS POEM IS . . .

The author of this poem
is as warm as the sun
her outlook is warm and funny
she is as sweet as honey.

The author of this poem
is like a flower growing
she's a lovely little bud
but only when she's good.

The author of this poem
is as cuddly as Pooh Bear
the author of this poem
has golden strands for her hair.

The author of this poem
is as tough as a tree
the author of this poem
is me!

Samantha Allcock (12)
New Wellington School

GARDENS

G reen leaves.
A pple trees.
R oses and rhododendrons.
D affodils and daisies.
E vening primroses.
N igella and nemesia.
S weet smelling flowers.

Helen Powell (11)
New Wellington School

THE BLACK FOX

The sky was dark and clear,
I heard the cry of the fox so very near,
I silently waited for her to appear,
Watching the grass and hiding my fear,
And then out of the mist came the wonderful creature,
Like a cat it stepped off the rock,
And for just one minute she stood as still as a block,
She ran into the distance and onto the creek,
And as the rain picked up I still did not speak,
Hoping and praying for the fox to come back,
Her white-tipped tail following her along with her pack,
They would sniff the air and dig to the ground,
And I knew that the fox would be my friend
And will always be around.

John McCall (11)
New Wellington School

FIRE!

Fire, fire, burning bright shooting sparks out through the night.
On that very fearsome night, the sky was going very bright.
In the distance far away, they were having a firework display.
The fireworks were going high, splitting clouds up in the sky.
Fire, fire, burning bright, shooting sparks out through the night.

Nicola Foster (11)
New Wellington School

THE ROYAL FAMILY

The Royal family are very important people.
The Queen is a very important person.
As she sits in her palace surrounded by jewels and gold.
Outside her palace she has camera men, the press, paparazzi
and newspapers waiting for her to come out.
Newspapers following her around day after day
not being able to have any privacy.
People knowing all her business.
As she goes out to places people shout and are eager to see her.
People clap their hands as they see Her Royal Highness.
As she wears her jewels and gold trying to get through those
everlasting crowds.

Lisa Sheridan (12)
New Wellington School

IS THERE ANYBODY HOME?

I thought it was OK, to go to the house,
It was quiet and deserted, just the sound of a mouse.
The staircase was creaky, some steps were missing,
In the distance I could hear some vampires kissing.

At times I thought it was haunted with ghosts,
Or fire breathing monsters that make you into toast.
That haunted house, I'd rather forget it,
For now just thinking of it, makes me regret it.

Christian Connor (11)
New Wellington School

MOON AND STARS

High up in the sky,
Moon and stars shine so brightly,
It's a dark blue sky.

A full moon tonight,
Stars surrounding the full moon,
No clouds out tonight.

Seeing them so small,
Looking through a telescope,
It all becomes so close.

Stars are twinkling,
The moon is going to go,
It has all gone dark.

Abigail Lloyd (12)
New Wellington School

STARRY NIGHTS

Stars are bright in the sky, they live high above us in the sky.
The sky is full of lots of dots just like little tiny lights.
In the night-time sky I can see all of the lights
in the big black fluffy blanket above.
The edges of the little
stars twinkle above.

Emma Prentice (12)
New Wellington School

MY STREET

As I look into my street,
I see a row of houses,
All with neatly cut gardens.

As I look into my street,
I see the children playing,
Football or tig, but whatever they play,
Each of them enjoy themselves.

As I look into my street,
I see car after car,
All shining bright after being cleaned,
By their caring owners.

As I look into my street,
I see people running round,
All in a fluster as they are,
Trying to get to work.

As I look into my street,
As it's getting dark,
I see parents calling in their kids.

As I look into my street,
I see the lights go out one by one,
After children do their teeth
Then get into their beds.

My street is such a happy place,
With children's illuminated faces,
Generally a happy place.

Kyle McGreevey (12)
Saints Peter & Paul RC High School, Widnes

CONSEQUENCES OF WAR

All I could hear
as I sat in fear,
was the wailing sound
of bombs all around,
shooting through the air.
I was shocked at the needs of repair.
I heard a cry,
so I decided to pry,
to see what I heard,
I saw a man with a beard,
he was in need of attention,
I did not have enough potential to help him.
I shouted for help,
I then heard a yelp,
I realised the man had died,
I just sat and cried,
I didn't know what to feel.
My heart could never heal,
'Why, oh why?' I said,
'Are so many dead?'
Little kids, adults of all ages,
No matter what anyone has sinned,
There is no need for a binge on bombs.
I dream of peace,
'Will the war ever cease?'

Victoria Jerram (13)
Saints Peter & Paul RC High School, Widnes

INNOCENT FIRST TIMERS

Their faces still haunt me
The faces of innocent men
Heading off to meet their fate
Not knowing what's before them

> Singing merrily, as they went
> Each one in a private's grey mac
> And every man leaving a family behind
> With a chance that they won't come back

Songs rang out from the barracks
Young men's memories from home
Perhaps ballads shared with a sweetheart
Or maybe a favourite of their own

> But the grim battlefields of flanders
> And the cold dampness of the trenches
> Took away memories of home
> And replaced them with corpse's stenches

The very best men died on those fields
Husbands, fathers and brothers
Leaving behind the best women
Wives, sisters and mothers

> My life changed forever that day
> But for others it didn't take too long
> To forget the men who died that way
> But I'll always remember the songs.

Caroline Murty (13)
Saints Peter & Paul RC High School, Widnes

JORVIK WALK

Imagine back when Vikings were strong
And York was so vile.
Smells of rotting animal flesh,
Human waste,
Muck on the ground.
Craftsmen working - using forefathers' skills,
To sell on the market.
An ugly cheap place
With makeshift stalls.
Infested with vermin of every size and race.
Pots, bone and cloth all get sold.
Each house is a farm, keeping chickens and ducks.
Home woven baskets store a weird concoction of things.
Families crowded around fires,
In rooms filled with smoke.
Food is revolting. Cereal, barley and oats are normal
And for Godly celebration pieces of meat wouldn't be amiss.
Fruit is common,
Rotting or not.
The communal toilet reeks of years of use.
Disease and death were hard to miss.
The street stretches down to the harbour
And wooden vessels dock here to sell foreign goods.
Although this town is not rich and they work so hard,
Fun and games can be found.
Checkers, cloth and other unknown items have been used.
Songs and poems from over the country,
Shouted while they quaffed their beer.

Chris Sutton (12)
Saints Peter & Paul RC High School, Widnes

MARCHING TO WAR

Helmet and rifle, pack and overcoat
Marched through a forest
With a lump in their throat
Guns over their shoulders
Boots on their feet
Fighting in whatever the weather
Rain, snow or sleet.

Scared stiff as the bombs fall
Tired and sleepy and sick of it all
Hiding from Germans in bushes and trees
The cold winter's wind is making them freeze.

The siren is sounding over again
Overhead is a hovering plane
Ready to drop a lethal bomb
When it falls I hope I'm gone!

There're many dead people on the floor
But soon enough there will be more
They've been bombed, frozen or even shot
Bruises, cuts, blood
That's all they've got.

Jane Goss (13)
Saints Peter & Paul RC High School, Widnes

A SHAME

Thud! Thud! Thud!
He fell, gripping his chest,
Then the blood came, what a waste of life.
None of it seemed real.
A nightmare I used to tell myself.

The man laid there on the floor.
Nothing could be done.
What had he done wrong?
He was an innocent one.
I never knew this man.
I slept near him, fought near him, I didn't know him.
Still I cried,
No reason, I just cried,
What a shame.

Karen Lynch (13)
Saints Peter & Paul RC High School, Widnes

CHOCOLATE

I know a place that only I know
It's full of happiness and chocolate galore.
Its name is Chocolate Street and it has many different sweets.

> The houses
> are made from
> chocolate.
> The park is made
> from chocolate.
> Everything's
> made from
> *chocolate!*

The chocolate people walk around and the queen of the land
is sitting on a high chair with a pink marshmallow crown.

At the end of the day everything disappears
until the sun rises once again . . .

Danielle Burns (13)
Saints Peter & Paul RC High School, Widnes

THE AIR RAID

It was nine o'clock when the siren went,
To the shelter we all got sent,
Everything was left behind,
Thinking of our possessions, what would we find?

We heard the bombs come whistling down,
In walks another person with another frown,
Another bang and a bright glare,
Is my house still standing there?

'Here comes the British Air Force,' heroic as they fly,
Blasting the Germans out of the sky,
The air raid's over but the same atmosphere's all around,
Everyone sad and worried, total silence, not a sound.

Chris Collier (13)
Saints Peter & Paul RC High School, Widnes

POST-WAR PEOPLE

Houses stuck together like soldiers in a row,
In the rain, shiny cobblestones glow.
Children playing in the street,
Dirty hands and dirty feet.
Doors are open for mothers to chat,
Upon the step they always sat.
The smell of chips in the air lingers,
Which would be eaten with dirty fingers.
At the end of the day the gas lamps are lit,
Tired old men come home from the pit.
Smoky old street and dirty old town,
He's worked all day for half a crown.

Lucy Kennedy (12)
Saints Peter & Paul RC High School, Widnes

Air Raid

The street looked damp with blood and tears
As I watched from my bedroom window,
Seeing the wreckage which the German's caused.
The raid was over, young children crying,
Searching for their parents,
Fire engines with their flashing blue lights.
People lifting heavy flags of concrete
To reveal what was beneath the rubble.
There were just two houses left standing
A horrified street watching
Whilst more and more were found dead.
Relieved that I was safe in my house
And not searching for my lost parents beneath a building.
Finally, the wail of the siren, we were safe again.
The street quiet again, empty except for a cat
Wandering across the street.

Mark Bevan (13)
Saints Peter & Paul RC High School, Widnes

My Perfect Street

I'd like to live in a street paved with gold
Where money grows on trees.
A place where everyone is happy
Where children play and dance and sing.
Everyone loves everyone and everything.
Cats and dogs would be best friends
And mice would be in heaven
Where people have enough to eat
And crime does not exist.
That would be my perfect street.

Joe Nanson (12)
Saints Peter & Paul RC High School, Widnes

The Smell Of Death!

We found an old dug-out drowned in blood,
Down in the darkness lay one sole soldier,
Whether he was alive, we did not know.

Out of nowhere came the whistling,
Down, down they came, then *bang!*
Luckily we escaped alive, I think.

Walking, walking don't know where,
No more food, no more rounds,
We came across a camp.

A ghost camp, a hundred or more dead,
None alive! They were German,
Swastikas, the German flag.

In the middle of nowhere,
Want to go back to the smell of English air,
Not the smell of death!

Edward Donoghue (13)
Saints Peter & Paul RC High School, Widnes

In An Air Raid

The air raid warning sounds in the dead of night.
All the people rush to their shelters.
The streets are all deserted
Just like a ghost town . . .

Then a noise breaks the silence,
It's a bomber!
The noise gets louder as it swoops down
And then a bang and a flash of light . . .

In the morning when the *all clear* sounds.
The people crawl out of their shelters.
And are greeted by piles of rubble,
Where houses used to be . . .

Everywhere there are sounds of people crying
And the unlucky few gathering their belongings.
Trying to find a place to stay
Then leaving their wrecked house - *maybe forever!*

Laura Jane Price (13)
Saints Peter & Paul RC High School, Widnes

REMEMBERING

There was a thick mist hovering low, the sky was stormy grey.
That's how I remember from years ago that terrible time in May.
I recall the dreaded air raids my family went through.
I remember the gunshots, the sounds - *bang, crash!*
I remember what I had to do!
I fought for my country
I sacrificed my life
I left all my children
My friends and my wife.
I was searching for adventure,
Instead I found fright - every morning, afternoon and night.
I look down on my home, my family and friends.
I think of the pain I caused them.
The suffering that never ends . . .

Emma Lewis (14)
Saints Peter & Paul RC High School, Widnes

FEAR IN MY KNEES!

Marching forward in the dark,
Not knowing what will happen.
Faces full of fear and doubt
Not knowing what will happen!
There's smoke from places which have been bombed.
Voices grunt *'Keep down! Make way!'*
Crawling through the bog, and hey!
Shouts of help are heard.
Up ahead - guns thunder
I stop and begin to freeze.
It's OK - they've passed
I carry on with fear in my knees . . .

Alexander Holden (13)
Saints Peter & Paul RC High School, Widnes

DEAD MAN'S CALL . . .

Orange sky lies over the trenches
swallows fly overhead.
Frost nipping at my fingers
I'm tired and lonely
I long for home . . .

Distant guns are still firing.
Shout and wails of men
cut through the icy darkness - the silence.
I'm unhappy and mud-splattered
I long for home . . .

Sparks light up the sky
like fireworks on Bonfire Night.
But no one's enjoying themselves now.
One young man shuts his eyes to sleep
he will never wake up.
I'm thirsty and in pain
I long for home . . .

I hear a shout and I lift my head.
A young man is running towards me.
'It's time to go now Sir!' he says.
I smile and close my eyes.
I'm no longer in pain or unhappy
I no longer want to go home . . .

Kathryn Wareing (13)
Saints Peter & Paul RC High School, Widnes

AIR RAID

People run frantically to hide away.
Grabbing all they can.
Running down those misty
Air raid shelters.
Lighting up a candle hurts your eyes.
Sitting there listening to the cries of people around you.
Wondering if you'll make it through the night.
You might fall asleep and never wake up
Or you might sit and wait for the siren to wail.
To say it's all over . . . until the next night!
People rise to see the disasters around them
And start to rebuild their homes and lives.

Ashley McGuire (13)
Saints Peter & Paul RC High School, Widnes

BY DAWN, BY DUSK, BY NOON . . .

By dawn . . .
When the new day is born.
The dew-wet tarmac glistens
The birds are singing but nobody listens.
The crowds are all in bed.
The cars are in the shed.
The street lies empty and stark
As the sun eats away at the dark . . .

By noon . . .
The midday shoppers are coming soon.
The street is far from bare,
As the shopkeepers sell their wares.
The lunchtime rush strikes
The shops sell their variety of goods.
From tins of beans to bikes.
The street is filled to the brim.
The shoppers looking anything but grim.
The rush in the street is one long race,
The look of joy and confusion on every face.

By dusk . . .
The tired and weary throng,
File out as the night birds begin their song.
The shopkeepers pull their shutters down,
And glance at the street, their foreheads creased in a frown.
The street is so unclean,
But the cleaners will clean it up with the Green Machine.
Night settles over the now clean street,
Like a dark paint-speckled sheet,
As the shopkeepers pull their curtains to.
The street prepares for another day of being walked on by *you!*

Holly Smith (12)
Saints Peter & Paul RC High School, Widnes

THE ATLANTIC CITY BOARDWALK

The Atlantic City boardwalk
Is a wooden road by the sea.
It is in the state of New Jersey
A place I would like to be . . .

The boardwalk is full of eye-catching shops.
The casinos are a sight to be seen.
You can gamble until you lose all your money
As long as you are over eighteen . . .

The Taj Mahal is a casino
It's painted very bright.
It's gold, white, pink and blue
It's a huge, amazing sight . . .

You can gamble next door at The Showboat,
You would think you were in the wild west.
We had lunch in their restaurant there
The food was simply the best . . .

People come from far and wide
Hoping to make a pile.
They put money in the slot machines
If they win, they will surely smile . . .

The other side of the boardwalk
The ocean is as blue as can be.
The sand is a golden yellow
And all of this - for no fee . . . !

Mark Chambers (12)
Saints Peter & Paul RC High School, Widnes

SQUEALING SIRENS

We sit around the table,
In silence and in fear.
At this moment in this time,
Nazi bombers will soon be here . . .

As I put on my uniform
I stand all straight and tall.
This war should end immediately
To the Germans it's a ball . . .

The siren hums through the night,
In the darkening lanes of England.
My family hurry, crying and scared,
Are the Germans yet in Ireland?

My face is all sweated out
As I run down the street to my job.
I wonder if all my work-friends are living?
On the road surrounded in blood, boss Bob . . .

I stop to help him stagger to work
I realise my life is in danger.
Will this happen to me? I wonder
As I stumble over a stranger . . .

My parent's home is blown to shreds.
I wonder if they're safe.
Why does the world bother with this?
But to me this war is an endless race!

Claire L Squires (13)
Saints Peter & Paul RC High School, Widnes

THE VICTIM!

It was like an empty box
no one around,
no one to hear my screams!

It couldn't be any worse
not even in my dreams.

A sea of dust covers my eyes
all I hear are gunshots and
bomber engines.

People with no legs, arms
or heads all around.
But me! I'm unhurt
not even a scratch!

Rubbled buildings now
like Pyramids!
Screaming kids now
without families.
Where will it end?
I don't know!

Will someone let me know!
I can't take it any more
it's driving me crazy . . .

I have no friends now
no family to turn to.
It's like I'm not even here . . . !

Craig Rogers ((13)
Saints Peter & Paul RC High School, Widnes

THE FINAL REQUEST . . .

As I sat down in our tent.
I took off my Dad's old helmet and threw it hard.
It made the sides go all bent
I opened my bag and took out the card.

Water splashed onto my bare head
and my uniform started to itch.
I ate half my ration of bread
and started to write to Martha and Titch.

I wrote to tell the loves of my life
Happy Christmas from Germany
And I ask you son and wife
as I risk my life - *never forget me!*

As one of my tears dropped on the card
the bugle started to blow.
If they beat us they must've worked damned hard
I realised it was time to go!

I got into formation
the bugle continued to blow.
I realised the complication
I was on the front row!

We started to shoot on that battlefield.
Then a bullet punctured my side
my eyes from the sun I had to shield.
At least when I die - I will have my pride.

A soldier called Sergeant Best
came beside me and asked
for a message for my family . . .
'*Yes! Ask them to honour my final request . . .*'

Craig Doyle (13)
Saints Peter & Paul RC High School, Widnes

THE TRENCH

As I sit inside the trench, I see men
Brave men - willing to give their lives for others.
Now I think back to when I signed up
I was excited, I was unaware of the terror of war!

As I gaze around I can see corpses of brave men.
Our Sergeant says to us *'It's nearly time . . .'*

Time to go over the top!
The rattle of machine guns.
The smoke of the grenades.
So I picked up my gun - ready to kill the Germans.
Even though I may get shot, I will die with dignity.
Protecting our country.

Then the Sergeant says *'Onward march!'*
As I peered over the top - I saw them!
The shallow-hearted executioners!
We all together paraded into the machine guns.
Man after man crashes to the floor.
Then there's silence . . .
On the Western Front!

Adam D Jones (14)
Saints Peter & Paul RC High School, Widnes

THE HIGH STREET

The bustling noise of the street
Is caused by the people who meet.
People buying and selling
Others talking and dwelling.
The street is very smelly
From the fish that feeds your belly.
The shops sell a range so vast
But not like in the past.
The transport is quick and good
From a shop selling sportswear
To a store selling wood.

Simon Duffy (12)
Saints Peter & Paul RC High School, Widnes

KNIGHTS AND DRAGONS!

A knight is gallant
the silver shining metal.
The Princess sobbing silently.
The sword with fresh blood on its point.

A dragon is ferocious!
the green scaly skin.
The cause of myth and legend.
Killer of brave men and women.

In battle they are deadly,
equal in every way.
But one must triumph on the day
that is the only way . . .

Andrew McCollin (12)
Sale Grammar School

LIVING ON THE STREETS

Cold, cramped, bleak and biting.
That's what you get when you sleep on the streets!

All the people passing you by
As if you are a dirty spot to be ignored.

No love in your life
No hope in your heart.
Every day is a continuation of the same old misery
Not knowing when it might end.

Loneliness and despair are an everyday occurrence.
When the next meal may be days away.
And danger lurks behind every corner,
Like a tiger waiting to pounce.

As the sun rises and shines its weak light.
You sit and wonder what you could have been,
Thinking of the life you might have had,
But it's all too late, as you're stuck in a deepening hole . . .

Adam Bolton (14)
Sale Grammar School

CLOWNS

Smiling faces, curly hair.
Big red nose and starry eyes.
They make you laugh.
Kids just love them, they love kids,
Have you guessed?
Clowns.

Jemma Ferguson (11)
Sale Grammar School

HOMELESSNESS IS . . .

H ow do you think the tramp feels?

O ut all day, out all night.

M aking a little money that people throw down.

E nd of the day, can't afford a cup of tea.

L ying in a box, dreaming of warmth.

E verything is a struggle, just staying alive.

S leepless nights, empty pockets.

S itting on a street corner, begging all day.

N o money anywhere, another worthless time.

E mpty pockets are often the case

S ome people are kind, they give you 10p.

S ome others ignore you like a piece of dirt.

I n the gutters is where you will sleep.

N othing left, life is not worth living.

T ramps everywhere, begging for money

H ardly anyone survives 5 years on the streets

E nough food for a week is a distant dream.

W ill people please spare change

O r these people could die

R ooms at hostels are too expensive

L ife is hard, and there is only one thing left.

D eath - which tramps welcome with open arms.

Vicky Fovargue (14)
Sale Grammar School

HOPELESS OR HOMELESS?

The sky is the only roof over your head.
your lights are the sparkling stars.
With frost as a sign of winter
and only a blanket to cover your scars.

Why should every night be the same battle
of trying to warm up every toe?
With nothing to occupy your mind
but to make sure your feelings don't show.

I feel like I'm just a memory
a bundle of forgotten hope.
Where once a life was living
but is now dying with no way to cope.

Inside my heart is breaking,
no home, outside I must stay.
The streets seem to be my only friends
they are there for me - come what may.

Although they are only a surface
for shoppers to trudge along.
The streets are the foundations
for me to build upon.

There must be a life around the corner
of my good friend - Baker Street,
Where I can realise my ambitions,
and get back upon my feet.

Rebecca Taylor (14)
Sale Grammar School

THE EMBRACER

The moon hung high in silken sky
as water beneath glistened.
She seemed to have been there eternally
as much a landscape as any other thing.

The silver light played on her flaxen hair,
her tear-stained cheeks as pale as wax
and her dress spoilt and ripped.
The clouds appeared, casting gloom
and with it their own special tears.
Yet still she waited there.

Far away, over hill and beyond,
her lover lay in the wood,
His arms entwined with an embracer dear
but not a woman as she did a-fear

This embracer was much more tender
and possessed her knight totallment.
As many a man was
clasped in stony bosom
asleep for ever more
alone in slumber eternal.

Tearful sleep
precious rest
ecstasy unending
pain beyond imagination
life forever good . . .

Still she waited beneath cloud and rain,
whilst above her in the restless night
braying steed and darkness cloak
enfolding all,

The embracer is abroad . . .

James C Robinson (14)
Sale Grammar School

WAR AND PEACE . . .

War is
wreckage
disaster and endless hope.
Scared people and frightened children.
War is just a glimmer of hope.

Peace is
life without fear.
A sunny day
Peace is always safe.

War is
dark
screaming sirens.
War is never safe.

Peace is
light,
caring and children playing.
Peace is nothing to be scared of . . . !

Chris McCourt (12)
Sale Grammar School

HOMELESSNESS IS . . .

Homelessness is when you yourself can't have privacy.
You have no friends
And no parents.
The solid floor beckons you closer
You can't keep it away.
It haunts you
Taunts you
Until you finally pass away.

On the streets you lie
With no money for anything.
Homelessness won't go away.
It's not a dream
And it will always happen.
You have no food or money
And begging is your last option.

People treat you as though
You are thick
And have no brain
You believe everybody is against you.
And you're all alone
Homelessness will live on, on, on and on
It will never be laid to rest.

David Meadows (14)
Sale Grammar School

HOMELESSNESS IS . . .

Being exposed to all who walk past.
Ridiculed by the world.
Being abandoned by your family,
Even friends look down upon you.
Oh well! It was to be expected!
The streets are your home now
And all who live there are your family.
I try to be positive, but it's hard,
Oh so hard!
Let me paint you a picture;
A picture from the soul.
Let it linger in your mind,
Whenever you walk past one of my people.
Pain, despair, loneliness, depression, homesickness and disease.
All words which spring to mind.
You will never know what it is like to endure suffering such as this.
But do not let me spoil your day.
Do not make me responsible for such a deed.
Just occasionally think of me!
When you lay in bed, think of me!
When you eat a meal, think of me - poor and hungry!
When you relax, feet up, think of me hiding behind the bins!
Hoping for people to pass me by, for people not to see me.
Reading yesterday's papers, telling yesterday's news.
Carrying all my belongings in old carrier bags.
Telling myself, when folk walk past.
'I am the same as you . . . just a little less fortunate!'

Charlotte Moore (13)
Sale Grammar School

WAR AND PEACE . . .

War is anger and pain
thunder and lightning.
Terror and death
people smashed under rubble.
Only ashes are left.

War is smoke and screaming
havoc and potential disaster.
Acrid gasses, an evacuated child.
Armies following their master.

Peace is a bright sunny day
life without fear and joy.
Races working together in harmony.
No wrong and nothing to pay.

Peace is a cloud in heaven
flowers swaying in the breeze.
A walk along a beach in paradise
and rainforests living - live trees . . .

Kate Ifon (13)
Sale Grammar School

WAR AND PEACE

War is fighting and killing,
War is anger and death,
War is hurting each other,
And taking your last final breath.

War is horrific destruction,
War is a living hell,
War is taking one day at a time,
And hoping it's not your turn to go.

But after war comes peace,
Peace like a warm sunny day,
Curing everyone's worries,
Then taking the pain away.

So stop causing arguments,
And stop causing pain,
Listen to each other,
Then look at the gain.

Nicola Williams (13)
Sale Grammar School

BONFIRE NIGHT

On the 5th of frosty November
the United Kingdom transforms.
from a joyful quiet place to . . .

The smell of gunpower spreading
like a really old bomb exploding
and the smell spreads.

The flashes light the sky
like a series of thunder and lightning bolts.

The different taste of gunpowder fills your mouth
like a drink of whisky warming your mouth.

The big sounds of banging wake you up.
Like the alarm clock early in the morning.

Your fingers get frozen like a cold December
like your arms being trapped in a freezer.

That's why the United Kingdom is transformed
on the 5th of November . . .

Andrew Martin (12)
Sale Grammar School

ANIMALS

I get up in the morning and look outside
I like to see butterflies flying by.
Birds singing in the trees
Caterpillars eating the leaves.
Squirrels running on their little legs
And I go to eat my bacon and eggs.

While eating my breakfast I hear birds
Mostly the humming birds - as he doesn't know the words.
My dog whose name is Martin
A big dog who is always barking.
Then there's Bilbo my pet cat
He's always staring at my rat . . .

Nick Richards (13)
Sale Grammar School

THE TRAM

The tram is like a speeding bullet,
When it starts up it is like a cannonball
It starts to race down the track like a missile
The sound is a horse galloping on a field
It feels like you're going into hyper speed
Then it slows down like the wind
When it slows down it is like nails on a chalkboard
Then it makes a sudden stop like it has hit a wall
Then the amazing ride is over.

Christopher Stephen Ashworth (12)
Sale Grammar School

TIME TRAVEL

What would it be like to travel in time
to meet your Mum before she was nine.
Would she be good or would she be bad
would she even like your Dad?

You could visit the nineteenth century
before they even had TV.
How did the children pass the day?
No wonder so many ran away!

You could go and meet Robin Hood
to see if he really was that good.
Did he rob the rich to help the needy?
Or was he really rather greedy?

You could go to the Jurassic age
to see the dinosaurs in a rage.
Watching Pterodactyls fly
like giant bats in the sky.

Moving forward to Tudor lives
meeting Henry and some of his wives.
Some were alive and some were dead
some didn't even have a head!

Leaving behind the days of yore
it's been quite fun and not a bore.
And as much as I love to roam.
There really is no place like home!

Catherine McQuade (12)
Sale Grammar School

WAR IS . . .

War is:
hate
death on wheels
hell on Earth
destruction!

Peace is:
children playing in the park
a breath of fresh air
a sunny day
happiness!

War is:
loss
starvation
fear
evil!

Peace is:
life without fear
giving
kindness
the sound of laughter . . .

Tom Bullough (12)
Sale Grammar School

WAR IS, PEACE IS?

War is:
Death and destruction before our eyes,
People losing relatives and hope,
Pain and anger mixed into one,
A crying child, not knowing what to do,
Fighting and killing,
War is a living hell.

Peace is:

Life and happiness,
A life with no fear,
Happiness and laughter all around,
Heaven on earth,
A hot sunny day,
Peace is a joyful life.

Natalie Snell (12)
Sale Grammar School

THE RACE

Listen to the wind
feel it blow upon your face.
Will we stand the pace?
In life's long race!

Wind howling in your ears
sun shining on your face.
Riding down life's hill
at an incrediby fast pace.

As my heart begins to start
with every fleet of feet.
The pace begins to pound
I can sense every sound.
As it rings round and round.

The race is nearly over
will it be a waste?
Or do I have it paced!
I need to sense the taste
Of win, win, win . . .

Michael Wilson (12)
Sale Grammar School

MY DAD IS FOOTBALL MAD!

My dad is football mad!
He plays for a team
And to play for Manchester United
Is his dream.

My dad coaches for a club!
And after, he goes down to the pub.
Last time he went to the shop
And bought mum a mop!

He watches football at breakfast
He watches football at dinner
He even watches it at tea
Then he goes for a *wee* . . .

Daniel Peet (11)
Sale Grammar School

SPORT

There is nothing that tastes as sweet as victory.
There is nothing that tastes so bitter as defeat.
When you play sport you will experience both of these
If you play football.
The worst sound is hearing the ball crash into the net.
It is like a killer blow delivered by a boxer.
The worst sound to a batter
Is the sound of the ball knocking the bales off
In sport, it's a risk you have to take!

Jim Skinner (12)
Sale Grammar School

THE SNOWFLAKE FAIRIES

Snowflakes are tiny fairies.
Oblivious to the naked eye.
They're made up in the heavens
before floating down through the sky.

They live in fluffy palaces
until the time has come.
Then they softly fall from their silver perch
and float down one by one.

Up in their magnificent palaces
placed high up from any woes.
They dance and play with sunbeams
and slide down bright rainbows.

Their faces blue and pointy
face holding a heavenly smile.
Their fingers like silver icicles
stretched full towards the sky.

After singing with the wind that whistles
their tiny feet touch the ground.
They either cry themselves away
or layer up into a mound.

And when the tiny fairy dies
its spirit is re-used again.
Made into another fairy
to float down once again.

Carla Rengifo (12)
Sale Grammar School

THE DESK!

A desk is a snapping crocodile
With its jaws of wood
Green and brown
The crocodile opens
When a child wants its teeth to write on
The *croc* snaps shut!

The *croc* sits there
Until the child wants to replace his teeth
Snap!
The *croc* rests
until the next day.
The jungle lights turn off
The *croc* sits in the swamp with its friends
And falls gently asleep, asleep, asleep . . .

Jonathan Whittam (12)
Sale Grammar School

A RUG

A rug is a fluffy animal
It is soft and cuddly
It is grey with thick strands of fur
It is so fluffy that it hides its eyes
A rug is a fluffy animal.

When you touch the rug your hand sinks into it
It is smooth and silky
It gives you a wonderful feeling
A rug is a fluffy animal.

Ciaran Farrell (12)
Sale Grammar School

SPECIAL NO ONE . . .

Tears drag down a tired, wooden face,
Telling a rusty past which once shone,
Of fear and sadness,
Deep sadness.
Her glass bones crack, as if being thrown against an iron wall
Of hate!
Her weak muscles cry out for forgiveness.
There she sits,
Waiting, waiting, waiting, waiting
For . . . ?
She seldom moves,
Her joints scarcely whisper.
Under-nourished, tired and still waiting
She forgets to live.

No longer does she sit there - dying.
She no longer feels sad.
She feels nothing
Her glass bones have finally shattered.
She just lies there
Her chest no longer moves, silently up and down
Her heart no longer struggles, valiantly to beat.
But no one mourns for her.
No one even talks about her.
But who would? She never existed to them,
The world carries on . . . regardless.

I'd just like to say, that she was never special, nor pretty,
But in a blank way - amazing.
She was a no one - yet someone.
I respect her . . . but I don't know who she was.

Rachel Forshaw (12)
Sale Grammar School

THE FIRST JUMP

The sun beats down on my back,
My hands grasp the rough rocks,
Hard under my feet.

Waves crash against the rocks below,
Noisy tourists talk in the beach café,
The sea shimmers.

Butterflies dancing in my stomach,
Clear blue sky,
Then nothing - *splash!*

The roaring of water in my ears,
I rush back up to the sunlight,
The water cool on my face.

Michael Jenkinson (12)
Sale Grammar School

LONELINESS

L onely as a lost sheep,
O ut in the middle of nowhere,
N o one to talk to,
E very day I think of myself as driftwood,
L ife just seems to go astray,
I t seems that years go by,
N othing breaks the sadness,
E nd is near, only surviving by the skin of my teeth,
S tranded,
S urrounded by a grey mist.

Emma Levy (12)
Sale Grammar School

THE SPIRITS

The spirits are happy, still and peaceful.
Everywhere is quiet, delicate and gentle.
The wind is blowing gently,
Whirling around the trees.
Hear the whistling of the wind, blowing a gentle breeze.
The sun is smiling, shining down on us,
Hot, bright and blazing.
The world is, oh, so quiet,
Peaceful and amazing.
The river gently floating downstream,
It looks so quiet, not at all mean.
Swishing, swoshing, splashing, sploshing.
Getting faster and faster.
Of the evil spirits, the river is the master.
The thunder crashes down,
Loud bangs all around,
The bright flash of lightning
Looks so frightening,
Hurricanes blow,
Tornadoes spin
Violent wind,
What a terrible din.
The world awakes,
The people scream,
There is an earthquake,
The world is so mean.
The spirits are angry,
It's not fair,
The spirits are angry,
Be aware!

Layla-Faye Bates (12)
Sale Grammar School

A PERFECT SCENE

As I sat in bed that night,
I dreamt about the most beautiful sight,
The trees were the most wonderful green,
It truly was the most perfect scene,
Another thing that caught my eye,
Were the beautiful birds that graced the sky,
And as I turned around I saw,
A natural delight, I looked in awe.
That sun beating down on a clear blue lake,
What a perfect picture it did make.
The flowers so colourful green blue and red
But as I lay there that night in bed,
I thought what we had done to the world
to make it like this,
A place that is so horrible that was once
such utter bliss.
The world it is a sorry sight,
Now it's a world where scenes like this
are only dreamt of at night.

Hannah Havekin (12)
Sale Grammar School

THE BOMBS ARE COMING

One day as the siren went off.
I was off down to the shelter with my mum.
My dad was running in his Warden's uniform.
I could hear the bombs streaming down.
I was wondering if my house had been blown out of existence.
I counted to ten and then had a look, I was still alive.
The all-clear went and out I came only to find my house was a
pile of rubble.

Lee Derbyshire (12)
Sale Grammar School

FAREWELL BILLY

We rescued you at one-year-old,
You were quite ill, we had been told.
You gave us sadness, you gave us joy,
You were our whippet, our Billy Boy.
We took you camping,
Playing on the sand.
With our other whippet,
You looked so grand.
The treatment you had was all in vain,
All it did was reduce the pain.
They say all good things must come to an end,
Thank you Billy for being my friend.

Victoreah Clayton (12)
Sale Grammar School

THE TRAFFORD CENTRE

The Trafford Centre is so cool,
it has lots of shops and a dolphin pool.
It has lots of cafes and places to eat,
places to look at and places to put up your feet.
I hear all the people laughing and talking,
looking around as they are walking.
The toffee shop has the most wonderful smells,
of chocolate and ice-cream and caramels.
There is China Town, a jungle and a place that looks like a boat,
and shops that sell wind chimes and candles that float.
I like the Trafford Centre without a doubt,
for your friends and your family it's a great day out.

Charlotte Atkinson (12)
Sale Grammar School

SHE

She sat there, alone in the corner,
Isolated from the people around her,
As if she were sitting in a corner with a pale, blue background,
Treated like she has some kind of disability.
Is she strange?
Is she weird?
Does her black hair and green eyes make her any different
from one of us.
She loves,
She feels,
*But yet she still hears them calling her names and
laughing at her,*
Even if she touches her hair or smell her perfume.
But to me she is unique,
She has her own personality,
Different but interesting,
Not dull and boring like everybody else,
She has a free sense of fashion,
Wears what she wants,
Doesn't care what anyone else thinks,
She fascinates me,
She is . . . she!

Jenny Gaunt (12)
Sale Grammar School

MEMORIES

As quiet as a mouse, she was sitting alone,
She flicked through some photos of those she has known,
A sparkle of fun was inside her eye,
Like a shining bright star in a dull grey sky,
Staring out of the window, she gave a small sigh,
Her eyes clouded over as she started to cry,
Slowly, so slowly, she tried to stand up,
Grasping the table, avoiding her cup,
She struggled to pull on her worn-out shoes,
And picked up the walking stick that she has to use,
I could see the arch in her back as she stooped to the door,
She can't afford glasses but her sight is poor,
She lifted a hand to open the catch,
And pulled the old bolt out of the latch,
The door closed behind her, with the key she fumbled,
And down the polished front doorsteps she stumbled,
She steadied herself on an old rusty rail,
Which just like herself was crooked and frail,
She turned to admire her beautiful flowers,
And talked to her neighbour of previous showers,
She walked down the road and got a bus,
And paid for her ticket without any fuss,
So lonely is she but so much does she know,
Her body is fading but her mind is aglow!

Abigail Wareing (12)
Sale Grammar School

AN APPLE

The Earth is an apple,
Floating around the fruit bowl,
Surrounded by unidentified flying fruits,
Always on the move.

Its crust is green,
Crunchy and crisp.
Its insides are yellow,
Pippy and thick.

A bite out of the apple,
Makes a volcano of juice,
While a breath of wind,
Makes it shaky and loose.

Aimee Skilton (12)
Sale Grammar School

MY UNCLE FRED

My Uncle Fred is a very bad man,
He cooked his wife in a frying pan.
He ate her with fish and beans,
Everything except her spleen.
The next day he heard his doorbell,
Satan was there and he took him to hell.
When in hell, they cut off the head,
Of my evil Uncle Fred.
All the evil came out through his mouth,
And it chased everybody out.
Now Uncle Fred is the only one there,
He burns all day in his rocking chair.

Anthony Leach (13)
Sale Grammar School

AN ANIMAL POEM

Apes act amusingly
Bees buzz busily
Chimps chatter cheekily
Dogs drool disgustingly
Elephants eat extraordinarily
Fish float fantastically
Geese gabble gallantly
Hyenas howl horribly
Iguanas itch irritably
Jackals jibber joyfully
Kangaroos kick keenly
Leopards leap lithely
Monkeys munch merrily
Newts nibble noisily
Oxen obey obediently
Parrots perform perkily
Quails quack quietly
Rabbits run rapidly
Snakes slither silently
Tortoises twitch tremendously
Unicorns urge unbeatably
Voles vaunt valiantly
Whales whine willingly
      X
Yetis yodel youthfully
Zebras zoom zanily

Melanie Meyer (12)
Sale Grammar School

THE SEASONS

Huddled up round the fire,
A white blanket covers the earth,
Children playing,
Winter is family time.

The beautiful flowers appearing,
Baby animals are all tucked up beneath their mothers' arms,
A different start for everyone and everything,
Spring is new time.

Heat for once in the year,
The best for me,
The sun is gleaming like a child's face on a snowy day,
Summer is happy times.

The leaves are falling,
Golden colours,
Silently squirrels scurry beneath the sands of sepia,
Autumn is thinking time.

Charlotte Higgins (12)
Sale Grammar School

WAR AND PEACE

Peace is,
Love,
Life without fear
A peaceful walk along the pier
Peace is life.

War is,
Evil
Terr ible as sin
A mouldy banana in a dustbin
War is death

Peace is
Wonderful
Life in heaven
A nice bike ride down in Devon.
Peace is heaven.

War is
Dull
Evil and vile
A tormented screaming child
War is hell!

Nick Bates (12)
Sale Grammar School

THE MYSTERIOUS FOREST OF DARKNESS

A sudden urge of fright as I approach the endless black tunnel,
Dark, cold, wilderness,
The howling of the trees as I stroll through the darkness,
The scurrying patter of little feet passing by,
The musty scent of the rusty moss,
A darkening dim light up in the misty night sky,
Mysterious black figures lurking in the shadows,
The bitter taste among the midnight trees,
Carefully and cautious as I tiptoe through the forest,
Not knowing what's ahead,
Not knowing what's behind,
A sense that I'm surrounded as I weave from tree to tree,
Brushing past the dew-covered leaves,
The tangled, deformed branches swaying with the wind,
Yet I still carry on wondering,
My heart pounding
Alone,
In silence.

Amanda Bradley (12)
Sale Grammar School

SICK

I'm lying in bed with a fever,
head throbbing, throbbing.
I feel so tired and low,
stomach churning, churning.
I'm bored with lying here,
throat burning, burning.
I can't eat or drink,
or do anything.
I try to read,
but feel too weak.
I watch TV,
but my eyes,
like deadweights, drop.
Then at last, I sleep.

Laura Newey (14)
Sale Grammar School

WAR AND PEACE

War is death
the baby crying
compared to peace
nobody lying.

War is sadness
the rationing of rice
and then there is peace
everyone being nice.

War certainly is
hell on Earth
and peace
when you can see the surf.

We hope wars won't last for long
and that all will cease
especially after singing this song
dedicated to peace.

Jonathan Millard (13)
Sale Grammar School

WAR AND PEACE

War is:

A living hell on earth,
A screaming child,
Deadly,
A destruction.

Peace is:

A life without fear,
A happy day,
Sunny day,
Life.

After war:

Rotting remains of people,
Black smoke covers the sky,
Rubble,
Funerals for all the dead.

Wayne West (12)
Sale Grammar School

SMELLS AND SOUNDS OF THE SEASONS

In the winter it is a time for Christmas
With the turkey, gravy and roast potatoes.
As I arrive home, I can smell the taste everywhere.

In autumn, the smell of fire burning reminds me of Bonfire Night,
The sound of laughter and talking, also the smell of candy.
On Hallowe'en the smell of pumpkins and cookies remind me
of fresh dough.

In summer the barbecue is laid out,
The chicken, burgers and chips.
The mouth-watering smell makes my hunger, hungrier.

In spring it is time for a fresh beginning,
The fresh breeze, the sound of the birds chirping and the fresh
scent of the newborn flowers.

As the year has gone past I can remember Christmas, Bonfire
Night, the barbecue and the new beginning.

The smells I smelt were turkey, burgers, candy and the
fresh-born flowers.
The sounds I heard were laughter, talking and the birds chirping.

Aqeel Bukhari (12)
Sale Grammar School

WAR AND PEACE

War is black, death and doom,
Tears and sorrow, dark and gloom.
The screeching sound of no return,
Death and dying, spoilt and burnt.

War is empty, screeching pain,
Cold and frozen, clouds and rain.
Ripped or broken, torn and tarred,
There's no escaping this despair.

Peace is blossom in the trees,
Blue tits, robins, honey bees.
Friendship, loving, nice and fine,
Flowers growing in bright sunshine.

Peace is heaven, kind and care,
Happy, tranquil, quiet and fair.
Smiling faces, a singing lark,
Peaceful breezes in the park.

Emma Swift (13)
Sale Grammar School

WINTER

As you observe winter at its work,
When the frost lays its web on each leaf,
And the snow falls down like a treat,
And the wind whistles as it beats upon the trees.

As the frost makes patterns upon the window,
He bites us by surprise,
And the snow seeps life from our gardens,
And makes it dull not bright,
As the wind ruffles our hair,
And makes us feel bare.

But when the nights get dark and cosy,
And the clouds shadow over,
When we sit with our hot mug of cocoa,
And Christmas draws near.
It makes us feel happy inside,
That winter is finally here.

Emma O'Brien (12)
Sale Grammar School

THE CHEF

As a chef prepared,
To cook a wedding feast,
He dreamt of what to cook.

The pots and pans whispered,
'When's he going to start?'
'I don't know.'

Swish, swosh! Went the stirring soup,
Bubble, bubble! Went the heavenly sauce,
Sizzle, sizzle! Went the succulent meat.

Fruit and veg smelt like heaven.
The food looked as fine as a summer's day.
Who knows the taste?

The finest feast,
Looked fit for a beast,
At that, a hungry one!

It was served up, course by course.
At the end there was a standing applause,
For the chef.

Gareth Cornelius 13)
Sale Grammar School

SHOPPING!

People suffocating me everywhere,
No air-conditioning breeze,
Sweating, sweltering, steaming crowds,
As busy as bees.

Bunches of grapes, clusters of diamonds,
Suits of clothes, packs of cards,
So much to see, so much to do,
But pockets ever empty.

Home at last,
Feet throbbing, arms aching,
Slumped weary into a chair,
Why do I do it? Why do I go?

Shopping!

Rebecca Stanfield (12)
Sale Grammar School

AN EMERGING STORM

The hour is midnight,
The sky is a black, velvet blanket comforted by the moon
and twinkling stars.
Little do they know a storm is emerging like a raging beast.
Suddenly a flash of lightning,
A bang of thunder, the clouds are creating war.
A wind is coming, growing stronger every second,
Bringing the waves along too.
The wind is here but is now a hurricane destroying anything
The waves are now demons as high as mountains flooding the town.
A flash of lightning, lashing out in anger,
Buildings crumbling.
The storm makes a whistle on his fingers.
Sirens wailing.
The town is like a trapped animal with no escape.
Has the black hole, which was a storm, any mercy?
The hour is six.
What's this? Silence!
No wind, waves crawling away and clouds clearing.
The sky is clear with the sun showing the way.
But the storm is still there, but for now, there's peace.

James Marrin (13)
Sale Grammar School

THE POEM WRITER

Last night I sat down to write some verse
I tried to write some for better or worse,
What shall I write about? I don't know,
A winter scene should be alright, with plenty of snow,
It would probably be cold on a winter's day
The problem is I don't know what to say,
The trees would be bare, everywhere would be white
I wish I could do this, I can't get it right.
The words won't come, whatever I do
Shall I write about some animals at the zoo?
I'm rapidly running out of time
Yet still haven't even written my rhyme,
I've been asked to improve this verse
I'm useless at this poetry, it will probably be worse,
I'll have to try and get it right
It's bound to take me all of the night,
It's two in the morning and I feel very tired
If I wrote poems for a living, I'd be fired,
My poem is no better, in fact it's dire,
If I said I like poetry then I would be a liar,
I'll look in a poetry book to give me a clue
I'll try to write about something refreshing and new,
I'm very tired, I'm half dead
Forget the poem, I'm off to bed.

Luke Adam Morris (12)
Sale Grammar School

IF I HAD A WISH, I WOULD WISH FOR HER BACK

She was my friend,
But she meant more than that.
She was family,
But better than family.
She was loving and honest,
But best of all,
She was my friend.

A warm, friendly, smiling face.
Listening to a kind and generous person.
Someone to talk to,
Who would listen understandingly.
Surrounded by a cloud of happy love.
Liz,
She was my friend.

Every day I think of her softness.
Smiling down at me.
Encouraging me,
And her two beautiful infant children.
She loved having fun,
And making people welcome
Because Liz was my friend.

She was my second mother.
From the age of two, my sister.
I really loved my stepmum,
But everyone has to go.
But why die young and happily in love,
From a year of pain and sorrow?
Liz,

She was my friend.

Eleanor Campbell (12)
Sale Grammar School

AN EVENING OF ACTIVITY

A conker dropping brown and ripe on the crisp ground,
The smell of a red flickering bonfire,
A brisk wind stood up whistling,
The ground crunches when it is frosty,
The stars are glittering like a bunny's eyes,
A full creepy moon, like white snow,
The owl hoots like a horn,
It swoops down and catches its prey.

The rain patters,
The mud slurps,
The worms come out from the moist underground,
Whilst the owl is high in the branches.
Silence,
The cloud covers the moon like a cloud of snow.
The world is dark.

The rain is stopping, the moon and stars shimmer,
The wind stands up and screeches,
The children's swing squeaks like a mouse,
The fox cubs come to hunt for food,
The owl silently watches
He hoots his horn again and the foxes run and hide,
But are soon back to root the bins.

They run away as the morning sun rises,
Dawn has arrived,
The screech of the road as people draw near,
The sun is warm,
The morning rush has come,
Leaving the night to trail behind.

Karis Leech (12)
Sale Grammar School

THE COUNTRYSIDE

As I arrive at my destination,
In a large, gasping beast
Of metal, churning, crunching,
I gaze into a view of colours -
A golden ball, shimmering
Burns bright and warm
In a sea of forever blue
Broken up only by a few floating
Balls of cotton wool,
Wispy,
Light as a feather.
Stretching into the distance.
A thick, lush carpet
Of emerald green and sunflower yellow
Waves in a fresh breeze.
Scent of honey, floats
Through the air, curling around my nose.
Buzzing wasps go about their playful
Mid-air dance
Dodging the low, swinging
Branches of a weeping willow,
Its blossoms, pink and ruby red,
Rustle, as a chirping blue tit
Grand in its coat
Of navy and cream feathers
Searches for a meal
In its home,
the countryside.

John Williamson (12)
Sale Grammar School

DISNEYLAND

The coach sets off, as slow as a snail.
Hoorah! We all give a cheer,
Off to France
It's the end of the year.

We sleep like a log,
Until we reach Dover.
The first part of the journey
Is finally over!

Over the Channel,
Through the dark of the night.
No more sleep is had,
Try as we might!

A sight for sore eyes,
Disneyland we see.
Lots to do
For my friends and me.

Carousels, roller-coasters,
Rides galore.
Sweets and candyfloss,
And much, much more!

The day is over
And off to bed.
Too tired to talk,
But dream instead!

David J Carter (12)
Sale Grammar School

MY FIRST TRIP TO THE ICE HOCKEY MATCH

A long time ago,
I remember,
When I went to a Storm match
And became an official member.

I was at the front
Watching Nipps
Doing tricks and stunts.
(My mum missed it, she was buying chips).

In the middle
Of the game
Whack! Smack! Thud!
The puck was a bullet, hit again and again.

The action was gripping
As the clock was ticking
And the score was seven-all,
Stuck at a tie.

The opposition got booked
For high sticking.
So it went on for a penalty
And extra time.

The player smacked the puck
And to the goal it came,
It went in,
We had won the game.

Then the buzzer came out
And gave a shout.
The game was over
And we all went home.

Matthew Parr (12)
Sale Grammar School

MY DAY

Tweet! The sound of birds singing in the morning
Bubble! The sound of the kettle in the kitchen.
Then the smell of coffee as I come downstairs.
Vroom! The sound of the hoover as I leave in the morning.
Ding dong! The sound of the doorbell as I call for my friend.
The smell of her house as she makes breakfast.
Tweet! The sound of her budgie as it flaps and flutters around
The smell of petrol as the car comes out of the drive
Gibber! Gobber! Giggle! The sound of children as I get to school
The smell of food as we go into the dining hall in the morning
Gibber! Boom! The sound of the teacher's voice shouting
The smell of food at break
Gibber! Gaggle! The sound of children as they go to the next lesson.
The smell of my sandwiches at lunch
Brrriinngg! The sound of the bell at the end of lunch
The smell of my new book straight and uncreased
Brsssh! The sound of the bus that comes late
The smell of cigarettes on the bus
The sound of cars as I walk the rest of the way home
The smell of tea as I walk through the door
Gibber! Gibber! The sound of the TV as I watch it after tea.
Shchscribble! The sound of my pen as I do my homework
The smell of soap as I go in the shower
Shhh! The sound of my dad's car
The smell of my dad's tea.
Click! The sound of the light switch
The smell of toothpaste.

Laura Bainbridge (12)
Sale Grammar School

ALL ON A MONDAY MORNING

Life can be like a big blue ocean,
People can be like many different plants,
But can you think how wondrous it is,
All on a Monday morning?

People will talk, people will walk,
People will wake, people will take,
It's like a storybook,
All on a Monday morning.

People can eat, people can beat,
People can stare, people can glare,
It's a never ending tale,
All on a Monday morning.

I can walk, I can talk,
I can play, I can say,
I can see how dull it is,
All on a Monday morning.

It can be happy, it can be sad,
It can be good, it can be bad,
Just think of the problems you've had,
All on a Monday morning.

Andrew Lines (12)
Sale Grammar School

WHEN AUTUMN COMES

When autumn comes and summer is gone,
The old leaves turn to a golden brown,
They flutter in the cool, fresh autumn breeze
To form a magnificent carpet of reds, browns and golds.

Some birds have long since flown away
To pastures warm and bright.
The trees are left alone and bare
On our chilly autumn nights.
Rustling leaves and crispy ground,
Twigs and nuts scattered all around.

The squirrels quickly scamper
Across this colourful carpet.
In their drays they have many nuts
Ready for the winter ahead.
No longer do the hedgehogs stir
For they are in a deep sleep,
Safe in their cosy dens.

The corn, wheat and rye stand proud
Like soldiers in the mist,
Caught with a layer of dew.

Oh, I love the autumn days!

Joanne L Curvis (12)
Sale Grammar School

THE POOL

As I enter,
The pool is a shimmering elegant carpet,
Screech! Like someone screaming down a foghorn,
I'm scared to jump,
So I crawl over to the edge like a snail,
I'm all alone in the corner,
Swish! Splosh! Splash! Like a sea in a storm.

My legs go down as a leaf does to the floor,
Faster I go in, up to my stomach,
Down up to my neck, where I am being choked,
I get trapped as if I am being held down
By the water.
It is like entering a freezer,
The water seems to have stood up and
Dragged me deeper down,
It is rushing towards me as a snake does
To its prey.
I feel as though I have just jumped into
Shattering glass.

People move away and the noise goes down,
Pshshsh! I'm all alone again,
Everybody rushes towards the changing rooms,
It's like a multicoloured carpet.
In the corner again, lonely and sad,
At the pool.

Chlöe Davenport (12)
Sale Grammar School

ANIMALS AND PEOPLE

Suddenly, the sights of butterflies came out of
The blue and were blooming in their nest,
And the bees were buzzing busily, angry and distressed.
People running free in countries far from me,
And others on the street with nothing on their feet.
I hate it when people fight, in the day and in the night,
And people getting hurt on the floor in the dirt.
I sometimes see rats being chased by all the cats,
And the green light to see cheetahs cheating, playing giraffes,
Whilst flies are sniffing the big brown cow-pat.
I've caught big yellow balls of fluff red-handed.
Running buffaloes down in the Bush,
And rabbits running fast from hares in a very fast rush.

Aden Brady (12)
Sale Grammar School

LIGHT UP THE NIGHT

As the jet-black quilt of cotton takes over,
The light becomes dimmed as the velvet, ebony sky drifts in
All the sparkling, shimmering stars glisten in the
gleaming moonlight,
The night is pitch-black, except for the magical stars
and the splendid gleam of the moon.
All that you can hear is the soft breeze of the wicked wind.
I lie in my cosy bed and the glossy moon begins
to descend leisurely.
As the radiant sun rises as sharply as a knife,
The rough night has come to an end and the
day has begun.

Jacob Robinson (12)
Sale Grammar School

D-DAY: THE WOUNDED IN WAR.

(Inspired by the D-Day Landings)

The tide washed up as red as a rose,
I feel my eyes begin to close.
Bullets fly, whiz past my head,
Then turn the living into dead.

The men and boys are torn apart,
By a force that stops the beating heart.
The bullets they do fly no more,
There're no more bodies on the shore.

The tanks roll up, the men run out,
The dying give a mighty shout.
I feel my breaths grow shorter, heavier,
The world grows darker, duller, quieter.

Now in my bed I lie,
And living I may be.
But there are parts of me that died,
Upon that bloody day.

It's only now I see a reason,
Why war should be fought.
It's not to stop life growing, but
Just to project it forth.

Hannah Robinson (12)
Sale Grammar School

FROZEN

An icy chill upon her toes,
Rises up her spine,
To her nose,
Almost in a straight line.

Her heart is a lump of snow as it stops,
As she tries to breathe,
But all can be heard is silent pops,
She takes her final heave.

She tries to fall,
But she's as stiff as stone,
She can't stand tall,
She can't speak a tone.

Her heart can't leap,
And she can't be sad,
She can't lie in a heap,
Or go completely mad!

She's like an ice-cube in a freezer,
She's so cold, she can't shiver,
Trying to solve the brain-teaser,
She can't even feel her liver.

Her eyes are frozen pools of water which are left open,
And when they start to water they are still,
She would die for some Alpen,
Not frozen by the chill.

But she is probably already dead,
She knows she isn't alive,
She can feel it in her head,
But it feels like a great beehive, *bzzzz, buzzzzz!*

She knows it's just the second and tries to take her last breath,
No use, she's found the sheet of death.

Nicola Kenna (13)
Sale Grammar School

THE RESTAURANT

As I looked at the menu,
I lifted my head.
My taste buds shouted out,
'What's that smell' I said.

The sizzling of onions,
The spitting of a steak,
Cigarette smoke like fog,
When the chefs take a break.

The baking of beans,
The roasting of lamb
And the sweat of the waiters,
Working as fast as they can.

The grilling of fish,
The splashing of oil,
The waft of a stew
Being brought to the boil.

This mixture of smells,
Makes my nose dance and sing.
I can't make a choice,
I will have anything.

Peter Flynn (12)
Sale Grammar School

YEAR EIGHT

Year Eight - the place to be,
English,
Art and,
RE.

Everything is fine for me,
Including,
Geography,
History,
Technology.

Ingenious mathematical solutions,
Science makes great concoctions.

French is fun,
University is near but,
Nothing is as good as a lesson in this year.

Tim Higham (13)
Sale Grammar School

WHAT COLOUR IS SPRING?

What colour is spring?
Blue like the true hue of the sky,
Green like the meadow scene,
Or pink. It makes you think.

What colour is summer?
Mellow yellow of corn fields,
Red like the poppies that bled,
Or peach. Reach for the summer!

What colour is autumn?
Brown like leaves that have tumbled down,
Gold you can hold for good luck while it's cold,
Or cream. You're not in a dream!

What colour is winter?
Snowy white like a child's kite in flight,
A grey gloomy day inside.
You'll look back and remember these days of black.

Laura Stewart (11)
Sale Grammar School

ST IVES

On my way to St Ives
I met Henry the VIII with his seven wives,
And each wife had . . .
Cats, rats and all researched SATS
Good old Henry was a believer,
One wife wasn't,
You should have seen her.
Squibly guts and lots of blood,
There was so much, there was a flood.
Wife number two was a witch,
Of course according to the snitch.
Yet again she lost her head,
Whilst asleep in her bed.
And now I'll tell you to calm your hives,
I never got to St Ives!

Michael Tose (11)
Sale Grammar School

TRUE COLOURS

Red is anger boiling up inside,
Waiting to burst like a balloon.

Orange is flames of fire dancing in the air,
Disappearing into the night.

Yellow is the bright shining sun,
Raising, setting in the sky.

Green is envy,
Jealously, jealously spreading across a face.

Blue is the cloudy sky,
Morning, night, afternoon, evening.

Purple is the colour of a flower in a woodland,
Swaying, swaying side to side.

Pink is rosy cheeks on a face,
Which has been taking in the outside.

Colours are everywhere you look,
Some are dull, some are bright,
Whoever you are; show your true colours.

Jenny Jones (11)
Sale Grammar School

WINTER SEASON

A frosty morning
all is quiet
in a seaside town
with no one around.

Amusements closed
fairground shut
roads half empty
only locals in the pub.

When winter's gone
and summer's arrived
no quiet seaside town
it's come alive.

Melissa Ferguson (11)
Sale Grammar School

HITLER AND DIANA - WAR AND PEACE

Hitler was:

Mean,
A racist man.
Who got joy out of whoever he can.
Kills, tortures,
Innocent people.
Greed.
Hungry to rule the world.
Because he thinks he's it.
When dead on the floor.
I'll spit on it.

Diana was:

Helpful.
Kind to everyone.
Seeing people who were sick,
To make them feel strong.
Helping to rid the world of landmines.
Helping to comfort.
Those that lose limbs.

They're very different people
One's evil, one's good.
One tried to destroy your neighbourhood.

Craig Mee (12)
Sale Grammar School

WAR AND PEACE

War is destruction and wreckage.
Peace is happiness and harmony.
War is sorrow and loss.
Peace is co-operation and understanding.
War is self-centred.
Peace is a happy community.
Bombs, guns and bangs.
Crashes, chaos and madness.
Air raids, planes and fighters.
War orders evacuation.
War asks for suffering.
Peace is innocence and purity.

Hannah Grimshaw (13)
Sale Grammar School

AUTUMN COLOURS

Golden leaves floating down from the trees
Trees filled with silver spiderwebs covered in dew,
Dew dripping off the green grass,
Grass covering shiny burgundy conkers,
Conkers hanging off the brown branches,
Branches being thrown up into the trees by children,
Children throwing the ripe berries,
Berries being eaten by grey squirrels,
Squirrels playing in the long colourful grass swaying in the wind,
Wind blowing the golden leaves along the fields,
Fields with black patches on it from the bonfire,
Fireworks, different colours light the night sky.

Callum Shevlin (11)
Sale Grammar School

WAR AND PEACE

War is,
Hate
Angry crows
Stormy black skies
Death, destruction, disaster

Peace is,
Love
Calm dolphins
Clear blue skies
Friendliness, peacefulness, fearlessness

War is,
Sadness
Angry storms
Red-hot flames
Sirens and screaming

Peace is,
Happiness
Light breezes
Warm sunny days
Children singing and playing

War is,
Bad
Peace is,
Good.

Helen Stockdale (12)
Sale Grammar School

WAR IS . . . PEACE IS . . .

War is . . .
Death,
Hell on earth,
Destruction,
Screaming children all around.

Peace is . . .
Silence,
Life without fear,
Life itself,
Without needing self-defence.

War is . . .
Demolition,
Bombs exploding,
Air raids sounding,
Evil all around.

Peace is . . .
Love,
Children playing,
School still on,
Everybody having fun.

Stephen Adams (12)
Sale Grammar School

HOMELESS

As I sit in my favourite doorway,
Away from the cold biting winds,
Surrounded by cardboard boxes,
Dreaming of the way life could be,
My stomach screams with hunger,
'Got any change?' I whimper.

Oh to be warm and cosy,
Sat by the fire with a bowl of soup,
Why did I run away
What did I hope to gain?
Nothing but loneliness, cold and misery.

Simon O'Driscoll (13)
Sale Grammar School

BONFIRE NIGHT

It's Bonfire Night,
The fire's burning bright,
Red and orange flames,
Are dancing, playing games.

Bang, whistle, crack,
Go the fireworks in turn,
They light up the sky,
Then disappear and burn.

Like mud, soft and sticky, is the treacle toffee,
The children still eat it,
While the parents sip coffee.

The fireworks have finished,
Guy Fawkes has burned away,
It's time to put the fire out,
Although we want to stay.

Mum says we can come back next year,
And do it all again,
We've had a smashing time tonight,
Shame about the rain!

Laura Kelly (12)
Sale Grammar School

WAR AND PEACE

War is . . .
Chaos waiting to happen,
A wailing child,
Sadness,
Hell on Earth,

Peace is . . .
Happiness,
People laughing,
No panic or stress,
Life being enjoyed.

War is . . .
Disasters, destruction,
Breaking up the earth,
Breaking up families,
Leaving them to hurt!

Peace is . . .
The world going round,
A beautiful sunny day,
Pleasure to all,
A child playing.

War is death
Peace is life,
War is anger,
Peace is happy,
War is guilty,
Peace is innocent.

Amna Bagadi (12)
Sale Grammar School

WARS ARE SUCH A TERRIBLE THING

Wars are such a terrible thing,
Killing people all over the scene.
People shot, bleeding to death,
My only hope is to see them rest.

All these families losing loved ones,
They've been shot by the guns.
The war is endless shooting,
There seems to be no end.

It comes at night, people scared,
They're all hoping their house will not be gone.
Planes are flying, shooting out the sky,
Far away you hear a cry,
Your only assumption is that they have died.

Daniel Bell (13)
Sale Grammar School

THE STRAY

I   was walking down the street,
T he poor shabby street.

W hen there at my feet
A puppy dog lay,
S habby and poor.

S trangely it got up and did no more.
T hen it started to walk,
R ound and round me
A nd I immediately fell in love
Y ou see!

Phillip Lamb (11)
Sale Grammar School

SICK

How is it when you're sick and you go to the doctors,
The doctor always shoves that light down your throat,
And he says 'Hmm yes, it's a bit red.'
Then he shoves the same light down your ears,
And says 'Yes a bit inflamed.'
Then he inspects your glands and squeezes your throat,
As if he's going to strangle you.
Then he writes a prescription.

On the way to the chemists your mum always says 'He was nice
wasn't he?'
But all he did was poke a light up your nose,
And when you get to the chemist and you are just getting over the
ordeal of being strangled,
You have to wait another three hours for your medicine,
And when you get it, it's awful,
But you know you have to take it,
Or you'll get worse and it will mean another trip to the doctors.

I hate being sick.

John Keane (13)
Sale Grammar School

THOUGHTS OF A HOMELESS PERSON

On the streets,
It's worse than you think.
God, my feet are cold.
Can't stay still gotta keep moving
Else I'll freeze to death.
Can't get to sleep, I'm scared,
There are bad people on the street.
Mug you, kill you,
Just for your pack.
I need a shower,
Maybe I'll sleep for an hour.
Beg for a while,
Give the people a smile.
I can't get a job,
Can't get a home.
Need some money,
Need some food.
Got no money,
Got no friends.
Haven't got time for trying to make amends.
I'm ill now,
I'll die within an hour.
Still can't get a bed,
Still can't get a shower.
Need to go now,
Into a sleep.
Hopefully a warm one,
In which God I will meet.

Mandy Evans (13)
Sale Grammar School

SICK

How is it when you're sick and you go to the doctors,
The doctor always shoves that light down your throat,
And he says 'Hmm yes, it's a bit red.'
Then he shoves the same light down your ears,
And says 'Yes a bit inflamed.'
Then he inspects your glands and squeezes your throat,
As if he's going to strangle you.
Then he writes a prescription.

On the way to the chemists your mum always says 'He was nice
wasn't he?'
But all he did was poke a light up your nose,
And when you get to the chemist and you are just getting over the
ordeal of being strangled,
You have to wait another three hours for your medicine,
And when you get it, it's awful,
But you know you have to take it,
Or you'll get worse and it will mean another trip to the doctors.

I hate being sick.

John Keane (13)
Sale Grammar School

SUNBURST YELLOW

Yellow is the colour of the sun,
the sun shines bright and gives off light,
that is the colour of yellow.

Yellow is the colour of the leaves,
the leaves of the autumn oak trees,
this is the colour of yellow.

Yellow is the feeling of happiness,
the feeling that everyone has,
that is the feeling of yellow.

Yellow is the feeling of warmth,
the feeling that comes from the sun,
this is the feeling of yellow.

Haydon Browne
Sale Grammar School

SALMON, WATERFALLS AND SCOTLAND

Up in the north the salmon are mad
People say they are the strangest type of fish
They leap and leap and leap all day
And fall back down the waterfall.

Salmon here and salmon there
Their silver skin flashes in the sun
They leap and leap but to no avail
They fall back with a splash.

They jump and jump with no success
I really think they should confess
They're useless jumpers and they should know it
They're useless jumpers: they always blow it.

They think they're great but they end up on a plate
In a Scottish restaurant.
They get taken from the water and given to a pauper
Far, far away.

Duncan Reed (11)
Sale Grammar School

A WINTER MORNING

I wake up in the morning
Look out the window wide
I get a cold and funny feeling
Just looking at the world outside
It's all so very silent
And looks completely untouched
Except for the small tracks
Made by the tiny thrush
I run across my bedroom
Open up my chest of drawers
Start putting on my winter clothes
And quickly run downstairs
Now standing in the garden
I'm surrounded by snow
I pick up a great big handful
Then throw it at the window
I run round and round the garden
And then I stop to see
No longer an untouched garden
But a mass of footsteps
Made by *me!*

Emma Needham (12)
Sale Grammar School

HOME IS . . .

Home is a place to be yourself,
A place for shelter and love,
Home is a place to relax and feel comfortable,
A place to be dry and safe.

Home is a place for warmth and security,
A place for food and a bed,
Home is a place for privacy,
A place to be dry and safe.

Home is somewhere clean and healthy,
A place to eat, sleep and wash,
Home is somewhere to see your family,
A place to invite your friends.

Beverley Brookes (13)
Sale Grammar School

CREATED BY MAN

As I watch the News at Ten
My mind sighs with deep thought
Shallow feelings stir inside
And hound my heart
Guilty, isolated in a world
Created by man.

The cries of pain
Sound through my head
No one's fault, everyone's to blame
Losing all faith in what was so real
Nothing is real, now
Death, darkness in a world
Created by man.

Someone should stop, sit down and talk
Why did this happen, didn't they learn?
Peace, quiet, calm, gentleness: seems so far away
Questions race through my mind
I find the remote control in a world
Created by man.

Christopher Dixon (12)
Sale Grammar School

WAR AND PEACE

War is death
A rubble of black remains
A sea of darkness
Remains of memories.

Deafening wailing
Lethal ticking
Choking smoke
No children at play.

Dead bodies
Falling debris
A smell of fire
Smoking black wood.

Peace is life
A pure-white dove
No more fights
Saviours of the war.

Happiness everywhere
No more crying
Children playing
A life of peace.

Family
No more fighting
A rose
Life without fear.

Nathan Gowans (12)
Sale Grammar School

WAR POEM

Planes flying overhead,
Flares lighting up the town,
Children screaming all around,
The sirens sound, so down
We must go to the old air raid shelter.

Bombs raining down,
Guns firing,
The sound of a plane crashing,
People's screams,
They're deafening sounds but they're all we can hear,
In the old air raid shelter.

The flames are bright against the dark night sky,
Orange, yellow and red they flicker and die,
You hope that the bombs stay away from you,
While in the old air raid shelter.

The raid is over,
So out we go, out of the shelter,
But outside there is,
Death, destruction,
Outside of the old air raid shelter.

So now we wait,
For the time to come,
When the bombings start again,
And that is when we shall trudge,
Down to the old air raid shelter.

Susan Phoenix (12)
Sale Grammar School

HOMELESS

You're walking around
With nowhere to go.
Aimlessly you try to find hope.
With no love, care or anything in your heart.
Your life is cold and dark.
You can see light,
But it's far away,
Maybe you'll get there some day.

You sleep where you can,
Anywhere will do
As long as it keeps the devil from you.
You're alone and scared,
With nothing to do,
So you sit there praying,
Hoping that God will give you a home.

You awake the next morning,
You've made it to the shining bright light,
Then you see angels,
Angels all around you,
Feel their hopefulness and see their happiness.

Then suddenly you realise,
God has given you a home . . .
His home.

Christina Galloway (13)
Sale Grammar School

HOMELESS

The snow and the rain, down they come
Where people walk past and treat you like scum.

The cardboard is soggy,
Need a new place to sleep,
There's not much to choose from here on the street.

The food from the bins, slimy, slush,
And the Day Centre's menu, is usually mush.

Begging for money, coins 1, 2 and 3,
I haven't enough money to get me some tea.

I miss my brothers, sisters, my mum and my dad,
I can't go back now I feel really bad.
Lying here now, I'm cold and I'm wet,
Leaving my home is what I regret.

Sarah Hudson (13)
Sale Grammar School

ISOLATION

Innocent screams of horror as you watch soldiers drop
one by one.
Solitary tears falling softly but deadly to the ground.
Overcome by fear, unable to move, feeling disconsolate.
Lost souls wandering, confused, drained, with
nowhere to go.
Aching hearts beating briskly, making sounds like rattling rapid gunfire.
Trapped innocent cattle
Immense fear grips them like fleeing animals.
Ordinary people, so much they have in common.
No one must ever forget the senseless, mindless violence of war.

Aimée Parkins (13)
Sale Grammar School

HOME

The sun beamed through the shop window
As if stretching its aching muscles,
Spreading its light across the land
And with it the old tramp awoke to another day.
His heart beating slowly,
As the cold crept across his body.
He arose from the cramped doorway
And started crookedly down the street.
He began to remember a time long ago.
When he and his wife had lived together in luxury.
He remembered his home, the place to relax
And enjoy its comfort and kindness.
Home, the place
Where you could put aside your problems
And be at peace with yourself.
Home, where you could sit in the comfy chair,
Relax and read the paper
Without a single care.
Home, where the stairs creak,
In places that you know.
Home, where the heart is
A place for you to go.
But now for him, these are only distant memories,
And as he walks down the street
Tears swell and trickle down his face, he's not sure
If they're from the cold or the sun in his eyes,
Maybe even the memories.
But all thoughts and tears
Are brushed away, to become
More and more distant each day.

Vicki Bolton (13)
Sale Grammar School

HOME IS . . .

Home is where you can be yourself,
Where you are looked after
So you're in good health.
You are safe and secure,
You can always be sure,
Of the people that are there,
That for you they'll always care.

Home is a place you can always go,
It is a place you will always know,
You know you'll be accepted,
In the worst of situations,
You know you can go there,
Without making reservations.

If all this was taken away from me,
I don't think I would cope very well.
The Big Issue I'd end up having to sell.
People on the street are very brave,
So for this reason, whenever I passed by
Some money I always gave.

Home is where you have privacy.
You can even bring your friends home for tea.
The homeless don't have any of this,
So I'm not quite sure how they can cope.
But probably by thinking,
There's always some hope.

Megan Blythin (13)
Sale Grammar School

HOMELESSNESS IS . . .

Homelessness is like a wall,
Trapping you in a world of hate.
You hear the same sounds every day,
But there you still have to lay.

Homelessness is hunger,
Being scared.
Too scared to get up, run,
But also praying you still have your life.

Homelessness is disease,
The world looking at you, 'freak' they think,
They're looking at you as if you don't exist.

Homelessness is lying, sitting in the street,
Silence lingers.
Remembering,
Remembering the days when you once had a home,
You could call yours.

Matthew Staniforth (13)
Sale Grammar School

HOMELESSNESS IS . . .

Home is a place where you can be warm and loved,
Where you can feel secure,
Where you can hear the familiar rustle of the trees outside,
Where you can be by yourself.

Home is where you can do your own thing,
You can step outside and feel the mild air,
And can smell the sweet smell of your home.

If I didn't have a home then I would be sad,
I would miss all the sounds and smells
That are familiar to me.
I am glad I have a home
and do not live on the streets.

Adam Turner (13)
Sale Grammar School

RIVER

River
Meanders slowly, twisting, turning,
Making its way through the hidden valley
Of forgotten kings, long past.
Warbling its way through the rocks and stones,
That attempt to stop its mightiness.
Powerful, strength, it grows more and more.
It thinks, is, can be.
Surging onwards, battling,
With life, creation.
Vigorously travelling
Beating the wind, beating the sky, beating the stars.
To surge ever forward, spiralling, healing.
Raging rapids,
Stopping suddenly.
Tumbling, tumbling,
Shivering, shivering,
Thundering, thundering,
Before all is calm,
Silent,
And the river returns to whence it came.

Natalie Vince (14)
Sale Grammar School

HOMELESSNESS

What is homelessness?
No shelter, no warmth,
No money to buy food - that means hunger,
No shelter from the weather - that means cold
Cold means fever.

When you ask someone what does homeless mean,
They reply - 'Dossers, squatters, tramps, outcasts, exiled, houseless.'
What is a house?
The dictionary says;
A fixed residence of family, inn, blood building,
Bed,
I have a bed, but I don't have a house.

People walk past,
Pretend you are not there,
Some drop the odd coin on your blanket,
'What will a penny buy?'
Some people say,
It buys a little food,
Food, only homeless would appreciate.

Every day is the same,
Begging,
Nowhere to go, no one wants you,
Nowhere to sleep,
When you find somewhere,
You can't get to sleep,
I hate it.

Kristy Lomas (13)
Sale Grammar School

HOMELESSNESS IS . . .

Homelessness is when you don't have a home,
Where you are not always welcome,
Where you are not always respected.
Homelessness is when it's dark and stormy,
And you don't have a bed for the night.

Homelessness is when you don't feel secure,
Where it's not always warm,
Where it's not always light.
Homelessness is when you can't spend time with people you love,
Because you're too busy begging for money.

Homelessness is when you don't feel like you belong,
Where you don't know where your heart is,
Where you don't know where to sleep.
Homelessness is when you haven't got any space of your own,
Where your bedroom is everybody's shopping street.

Homelessness is when you don't feel well,
When there's nobody to care for you,
If anybody cares at all!
Homelessness is when you can't have a bath,
Where you can't stay clean.

Homelessness is when you realise,
How much you miss the small things you took for granted,
When you wish you were back at home.
Homelessness is when you live on the streets
And you have nowhere else to go.

Katie Mackenzie (13)
Sale Grammar School

HOMELESSNESS

This place, is a dying world, from where I can see no escape,
And as I lie down, my thoughts surround me,
And carry me to my mind's eye.

The wind is blowing hard, like pangs of pain,
Sweeping through my body from head to toe
And the rain falls, like distant memories.

And as I slouch down in the corner,
I think about yesterday,
What I had and what I've lost,
And the tears pour from my eyes.

So here I am, all alone, I feel like I'm falling, falling
Down and down into the deep murky abyss.
I look around for you, but you're not there.

What is a home? I keep on asking,
And I hear the green leaves on the trees whisper, home is love.

I have nothing to lose now, not even my pride,
And I hope that when I pull this trigger,
There will be a home for me in heaven.
I'm dying, I'm falling, into your arms which are like a temple
I'm dead, I've fallen, no longer the cold and lonely
The timid or the frail.

Andrew Kenyon (13)
Sale Grammar School

ON THE STREETS

As the sun goes down,
I sit and stare
At the stars in the sky,
And at the lights of the town.
Alone, alone, alone.

As the sun comes up,
I sit and stare
At the clouds in the sky,
And at the people in the town.
Alone, alone, alone.

As the day goes by,
I sit and stare
At the sun in the sky,
And at the shops in the town.
Alone, alone, alone.

As night comes again,
I sit and stare
At the ten pence in my hat,
And at my cardboard box.
Alone, alone, alone.

As day comes again,
I sit and stare
At my old tattered sign,
And at Tuesday's papers.
Alone, alone, alone.

Helen Niblock (13)
Sale Grammar School

HOMELESSNESS IS . . .

Homelessness is not having warmth or security,
Not having a place to go,
People turn you away, as if they are better than you,
Like you're an animal,
They don't respect you.

Homelessness is being cold and on the streets,
Wanting a large, filling cooked meal,
But you have no money to pay for one,
You feel hungry and cold.

And when the winter comes,
And you've got no money or a warm bed to sleep in,
You want somebody to cuddle up to,
Someone to love,
But no one wants you.

They don't see you for who you are,
They see you as a no one,
A dirty, old tramp,
Worthless.

Mark Watterson (13)
Sale Grammar School

BASKETBALL

Saturdays are basketball days
I rise up as early as the sun
Get dressed as quick as a shot
Waiting for my dad
He can be as slow as grass growing, sometimes.

We pick up Adam on the way there
He's still a sleepy bear.
The rest of the team are already there
Waiting for the match to start.

The whistle blows and we begin
David jumps as high as a helicopter
Adam passes, strong as a bull
Ryan runs as fast as a whippet
Paul scores as true as you and me.

In the end we win
We shake hands
We go home as happy as a rabbit with a carrot.

Harry Pettener (11)
Sale Grammar School

ME, MYSELF AND I

Me - as I walk to and from school every day.
I cross the 'reck' - as everyone calls it, recreational ground,
I walk on rough, dew-soaked grass,
I watch the trees sway slowly in the breeze.
The scenery changes to a contrast.
Myself - creeping through a dark, damp alley,
Coated in glass, broken and smashed-up bottles,
Rubbish coats the muddy floor.
Spray-painted walls, graffiti on brick with words and pictures
which have no meaning to me.
The scenery changes yet again.
Houses are along the country road,
Horses in an enclosure, gently lapping up water,
And there are gardens containing an array of colour,
Lining the streets.
Me, myself and I.
My life.

Caroline Hirst (14)
Sale Grammar School

HAVE YOU EVER?

Have you ever tasted . . .
A fresh sugary doughnut
At a funfair?

Have you ever tasted . . .
Salty french fries
Dipped in ketchup?

Have you ever tasted . . .
A crisp toasted sandwich
Oozing cheese?

Have you ever tasted . . .
A freshly picked apple
From an English orchard?

Have you ever tasted . . .
A slimy slug
Hiding in your lunch!

Alex Bingham (11)
Sale Grammar School

AUTUMN DAYS

My golden leaves used to confine me,
They used to keep me warm.
But now they have deserted me,
Left me cold and all alone.

They glided down to earth,
Like birds just learning to fly.
Now they lie on the grass,
Gazing up at the sky.

Helen Hardwick (11)
Sale Grammar School

SICK

The night has come, alone again I shiver in my bed.
Shh! Shh! Mustn't wake anyone.
The room, so distant, everything a mile away.
The noise of traffic, like a crescendo,
Louder, louder.
Until nothing.
Just a droning, buzzing in my brain,
Present like a heart monitor recording no pulse.
I check mine.
I'm still alive.
I drift again into an uncomfortable restless sleep.
The fever relentless,
Its tenacity amazes me.

Awakened, the smell of food makes my throat wretch.
The muttering voices downstairs are a comfort,
Unlike the constant shooting pains filling my head.
Any effort at a shout remains as a whimper.
Will I recover?
Or
Should I recover?
This familiar question churns in my mind,
As my immunity reduces.
Another day off school I decide,
One more won't hurt!

Sarah Mills (13)
Sale Grammar School

SANTA CLAUS

Santa Claus has come to town,
the fun has just begun.

The snowflakes fall from town to town,
and now there is no sun.

His big red suit with his shiny belt
glows up from miles away.

He travels around from house to house,
on his reindeer-flying sleigh.

He's never early he's never late
he's always just on time.

He never waits to hang around,
so everything's just fine.

The time has come for Santa to go,
and have a game of golf.

Let's say goodbye to Vixen, Prancer and Blitzen
and Dancer and last of all Rudolf.

Kirsty Ferguson (13)
Sale Grammar School

WINTERTIME

The winter is snowy and cold and white,
short is the day and long is the night,
we lie in our beds all cosy and warm,
while the night gives way to a frosty morn.
When do the days start to get light?

Katy Warburton (11)
Sale Grammar School

THE LAST DRAGON

Forgotten fighter
In depths of whispering woods.
I saw you there, faded far away, dissolved in time.

Hide in all your glory old
And leave this day unseen.
For racing skies, for knights with thrusting swords
And bloodstained armour in burning battles belong to ages gone.

And all you do is reminisce of days with dream-like qualities
And savour in your once feared might.

Your eyes they do not see, but reflect what might have been.
You hear only the drum of victorious fights and the smell of
                                                    foolish blood.

Behold your fiery temper, your webbed wing.
I marvel at your sunburnt tongue, your mosaic scales,
Your splintered feet, all growing old
Under the weakening eye of the day.

Yet I am sure
You were not born for death, dear immortal dragon,
My mythical magician
Sure to rise again.
In the shadows of your distant mind
A monster lurks, a colossal beast.

Yet now in your simplicity you sleep.

Lara Wood (13)
Sale Grammar School

FREEDOM TO BE OR FREEDOM TO STAY

A man ran energetically through the tall, claggly grass
under the pitch-black night sky.
His goal, to retrieve the object his master had dropped,
His master craved it, needed it, would not live without it,
But the master would only lose it again and he would have
to run like the wind to bring it back into their power,
Trees encompassed the field casting long shadows
blacking out his only view,
But he had to reach it,
There it was, lying on the ground, camouflaged into the nature around.
He reached down and scooped it up swiftly in his jaws,
His teeth, slotting into the marks they had previously made,
He turned, his master was in sight, he ran again speedily
back to his master.
He toyed with it for a while and then passed it to his master,
His master gripped the object in his paws and then once again,
as before . . .

. . . he dropped it.

Miles Haslam (13)
Sale Grammar School

NIGHTMARE NEIGHBOURS

Look at this:
What have we here?
It's an empty can of beer.
What's its purpose, why's it there?
I wonder who's it was.
If you've played your music loud,
or invited round a crowd,
you can bet your life
or pet or wife
that Kate will know the details.

Can you hear the Dobsons?
They're the ones next door.
While Natalie is screaming,
the boys kick down the door.
Their parents don't control them,
or keep them on a lead,
their dad plays on his drum kit,
that isn't what we need.
He and his wife are really quite nice,
it's a pity they had to breed!

Jenny Reed (13)
Sale Grammar School

A DREAM

The dream I had was extra weird
It had a world that wasn't feared
That had fish in the sky and dogs in the sea
We had breakfast for dinner and dinner for tea
Objects were living and were alive
Birds couldn't fly but they could do a jive
Children no longer loved to play at the park
It was called day when it was still dark
Humans could bark but could not talk
Red and white fish could get up and walk
We ate lemonade and drank up our nose
And didn't use our fingers we used our toes
Elephants were small and hamsters were big
Cats could dance and moles couldn't dig
Walls were floppy and jelly was hard
Nothing whatsoever needed a guard
The grass was blue and the sky green
No one could be horrible nasty or mean.

Lisa Rushton (13)
Sale Grammar School

THE SUN

As morning begins the sun slowly peeps,
From beneath the clouds that surround it in its sleep.
The vibrant colours that begin to glow,
Are already now beginning to show.
And as the sun rises over the valley's lake,
The people now are beginning to wake.
So splendid and bright,
It fills their rooms with a shower of light.
So distant, yet so near,
It seems without a care.
So quick and elegant it leaps across the sky,
For it knows it soon must say goodbye.
And as the day begins to end,
It knows it soon must start to descend.
So slowly without a sound,
It silently slips beneath a cloud.

Kerry Proctor (13)
Sale Grammar School

FRED THE DRAGON

I am Fred the dragon
I never meant any harm
I'm a big clumsy dragon
Ow, I just burnt my palm.

I am Fred the dragon
I never meant any harm
Why do they keep hassling me?
They really have no charm.

I am Fred the dragon
I never meant any harm
I just plod about
Acting very calm

I am Fred the dragon
I never meant any harm
I'm being slayed right now
By that big guy from the farm.

Daniel Brook (13)
Sale Grammar School

STARRY NIGHT

Whoosh, bang, crack, screech!
Rockets at twenty pounds each
Exploding with a whooshing sound
Leaving a pattern so high and so round.

Chinese firecrackers nailed to a stake
Making all our ears ache.
Catherine wheels screeching like a banshee's wail
All of us hoping the fixing won't fail.

Mount Etna's erupting like volcanoes
Giving a series of vivid glows.
Crackers burning oh so bright
Bathing the trees in a beautiful light.

The fireworks have ended, sparklers remain
Spraying out their silvery rain.
The sparklers give the animals a fright,
The fireworks added more stars to the night.

Thomas Christie (12)
Sale Grammar School

SICK

My head is throbbing more and more.
It can mean only one thing:
    I'm sick,
    I'm ill.
Days of torture are creeping my way,
Throwing themselves into a horror movie,
Which has insisted on replaying round my mind.
Headaches which throb more and more,
Sore throats which scuffle and scratch every time I swallow.
Noses which are blocked up, unable to breathe in the air
which I so desperately need.
Muscles which feel like jelly are reluctant to stand up and walk.
    Bang!
    Bang!
The noise won't leave me alone
Pain is dinging on.
Laughing endlessly like a bully, teasing an innocent victim.
A sneeze gets out of my body,
Poisoning the bed I am lying on.
Is there anything I can do?
I will just have to despair in the torture of the week.

Helen Wolstenholme (13)
Sale Grammar School

COLOURS OF AUTUMN

Orange and brown are the leaves falling,
Brown are the conkers on the floor,
Black is my new school uniform,
Brown are my boots by the door.

Sarah Ollier (12)
Sale Grammar School

SPRINGTIME

Yellow daffodils growing in my garden
The bright sun shining on us and the sky is getting clearer by the day.
Little white lambs just born,
And blue tits singing in the trees.
Green grass freshly cut,
The flower buds are about to turn pink.
There are Easter eggs on the table ready for me to eat.
My mum is getting me and my sister lots of new clothes.
Ripe strawberries are turning red,
And pears are nearly ready to be picked off the trees.
I'm packing my holiday clothes,
Because summer is just around the corner.

Lisa Chan (12)
Sale Grammar School

SPRING

Fresh air, trees, daffodils,
this is spring,
the feeling inside me
it's like the warm glowing cinders
                    of the old winter fire.

The weather, sunny, nice,
gets rid of the horrid cold in the winter,
it takes my breath away,
with the light breeze in the air.

Waiting for summer,
travelling through my favourite season,
hoping it will last forever.

Wayne Francis (13)
Sale Grammar School

RAINBOW

Red is the colour of anger
Red is burning deep.

Orange is a flicker in a fire
Orange is the colour of your desire.

Yellow is the colour of the sun
Yellow is a blasting gun.

Green is the colour of envious eyes
Green is the colour of stormy skies.

Blue is the colour of a beautiful ocean
Blue is the colour of a burbling potion.

Indigo is a bruise on a hurt arm
Indigo is the colour on a hurtful face.

Violet is the colour on a brass band's face
Violet is the colour of an important case.

Rainbows bring many happy smiles,
Rainbows go on for miles and miles,
There's a rainbow in everyone.

You don't have to go far to
          find one.

Kate Gibson (11)
Sale Grammar School

CARS

Most people like cars.
But not when it's their pa's.
The bodywork so old
And the interior so cold.
The wing mirrors so rusty
And the seats so dusty.

When you get your dream car
Nothing like your pa's.
With its windows so clear,
And with its cup holder for beer.
The bodywork so unrusted,
It's so easy to get busted.

Nicholas Alderson (11)
Sale Grammar School

SNOW!

Winter is here, hooray!
There'll be snow and I can play!
But look, it's boring and grey!
And where is the snow, anyway?

I turned away from the window,
And decided to go up to bed,
'When you wake up tomorrow,
You'll feel better,' at least that's what Mum said.

When I woke in the morning,
What a wonderful sight!
The whole of our back garden
Was covered in a blanket of white!

I ran down the stairs,
Threw on scarf, gloves and hat,
Rushing about
Nearly stood on the cat!

I threw open the door and there I stood,
It was like a glittering fairytale wood,
Here come my friends, I'm off to play,
Winter is here, at last, hooray!

Emma Hawkins (11)
Sale Grammar School

JANUARY'S CHILD IS WET AND WINDY

January's child is wet and windy,
February's child is cold and misty,
March's child is cheerful and chatty,
April's child is small and delicate,
May's child is warm and joyful,
June's child has ambition,
July's child is free and wild,
August's child is hot and sultry,
September's child is cool and hip,
October's child is fresh and mild,
November's child is foggy and dull,
And the child that's born in the 12th month is a gift to the
                                        world like all the rest.

Hannah Coffey (11)
Sale Grammar School

KALEIDOSCOPE

Endless swirling psychedelic colours,
Ensnaring the lonely traveller in those coloured lands,
Folding, intertwining with glowing synthesising rays,
Perfectly constructed symmetry of illuminated forms,
Wonderfully created buildings of geometrical light,
Formations of splendour,
Amounting to the ultimate model before
                          Destruction.

Daniel Rushton (13)
Sale Grammar School

THE TREE

It sways in the autumn breeze
And looks so nice, just standing there,
The leaves are starting to fall
And the berries are ripened and fresh,
It just keeps on swaying in the breeze.

It sways in the winter breeze
Just standing in the freezing cold,
There are no leaves on the tree, it is so bare
And the birds have nowhere to rest,
It just keeps on swaying in the breeze.

It sways in the spring breeze
With all the blossom blooming,
All the leaves are coming back
And the birds can rest,
It just keeps on swaying in the breeze.

It sways in the summer breeze
With all the leaves back on the trees,
The birds are making all their nests
For their babies to rest,
It just keeps on swaying in the breeze.

It sways the whole year through
Come rain, snow or sleet,
The leaves come off, then they return
The following season,
It just keeps on swaying the whole year through.

Lucy Connor (13)
Sale Grammar School

MATCH DAY

It's match day!
City play United later today
The fans will be shouting
While the tension is mounting
Who will win later today?

I have my bacon butty
Then I'm off to watch the footie
I'm at the ground for twenty to three
Where my mate Bob is waiting for me

Just ten minutes into the game
Giggsy scores with a perfect aim
The fans went wild
But one hit a child
One-nil to United, hooray!

In the second half
Beckham pulls his calf
The City fans were delighted
Unlike Man United
Five minutes later
Dickov punched a spectator
He was shown the red card
His punch looked rather hard

But near the end
City scored two
This all happened while I was on the loo
I heard it was Dickov and Bradbury too
Of course this had to happen when I was on the loo!

Michael Stockley (11)
Sale Grammar School

SCHOOL AGAIN

I wake up, ahhh!
Horror it's school today.
It's half past eight already,
I jump into my clothes,
Scoff down my breakfast
And run to school as fast as
my little legs can carry me.

My first two lessons,
Horrible history and
Tortuous technology,
Then brilliant break.
The bell rings,
No! It's scary science,
Then the raging RE teacher.
Wait the teacher isn't here,
We are going to do
Monstrous maths instead.

Lunchtime *No! No! No!*
Mushy peas and
burnt sausages.
Then a bottle of pretty
warm water.

The bell rings, it can't be!
It's man-eating music,
One more lesson and
it's the worst.
Gruelling games,
Forty-five minutes here we come,

Hooray home time!

Michael Heap (11)
Sale Grammar School

WILD WEST SHOOT-OUT

In the tavern the lights were low,
What was outside no one wanted to know,
It was Dirty Dan up to his deeds,
Robbing the bank, treating people like weeds.

Then came the sheriff,
Puffing his cigar,
He turned to Dan and said,
'I'm the good guy by far.'

Dan shot to the sky to scare the birds away,
Ten steps then shoot,
'I'll beat you any day!'

The first step was slow,
The second was quicker,
The rest were fast,
And then the blast.

Dan fell to the floor,
With a mighty crash,
The sheriff had won,
And all to be heard was the tavern sign swinging in the sun.

Robert Buckley (11)
Sale Grammar School

HALLOWE'EN NIGHT

It's Hallowe'en night and the stars are shining bright.
The witches are out and the children are too.
It's half past two, in Coohoo Lane,
They're all dressed up like cats and bats.
Walking around in the light of the moon.

Corrie Finn (11)
Sale Grammar School

THE FLU

I opened my eyes,
And to my surprise,
The room around me was spinning.
I got out of bed,
The pain in my head,
Told me my alarm bell was ringing.

I shouted to Mum,
To hurry and come,
As shivers ran through my body.
My temperature's hot,
But my body is not,
My throat is dry and is aching.

Is it the flu?
I wish I knew,
My body is aching all over.
Then Mum entered the room,
And wrapped me in a cocoon,
Of blankets, love and affection.

Katie Hemmings (13)
Sale Grammar School

COLOUR

Red is for anger and hatred burning up inside me,
Orange is when I am back in control,
Yellow is the feeling when I am totally calm.
Green is for the first breath of spring,
Blue is when I am filled with joy,
Indigo is when I feel like falling asleep,
Violet is the colour of the room I sleep in.

Daniel McCauley (11)
Sale Grammar School

MY DAILY SCHOOL RECIPE

Take at least one thousand children,
And slowly sprinkle them around a very large school,
Add shouts and scraping of chairs,
And watch the children simmer into pupils.

When the end of lesson bell rings,
You should be able to smell the science block,
And faintly smell the smell of burning rubber,
And shouting teachers.

As children walk past the head teacher's office,
Add four lost children and a crying child,
Followed by a steaming and furious teacher,
With burnt hair and burning clothes,
Now add the final touch.

The last thing to add,
Is a burning school bus,
Filled with chewing gum,
And now you have my daily school recipe.

Andrew Waring (11)
Sale Grammar School

SICK

I hear muffled voices
Catch glimpses of faces
People crowded around the bed where I lie.

It's as if it's not actually me in the bed
I feel myself floating above it
I look down and see them, their long worried faces
I look thin and pale, yet almost peaceful.

The doctor said that if I survive the night
The fever should go, I'd get well again
That's why they're all here, holding their breath
Waiting to see if I live or die.

I twist and turn through the night, while the dawn grows nearer
I mumble something in my restless sleep
The colour returns back to my cheeks
The fever has gone, everyone breathes a sigh of relief.

Leonie Ratty (13)
Sale Grammar School

TRAPPED

Down in a hole deeper than deep,
There we sat while others were asleep.
We were all black from the mud and rain,
We were all in tears of pain.

> I started to imagine that it was all just a dream,
> But when I opened my eyes I could still hear the stream.
> I could just see the stars from the greatest pit,
> Then I decided to die and to quit.

Just when I was about to die,
I saw a yellow tie.
Then I heard someone shouting,
And we all started jumping.

> No longer were we *trapped!*

Rebekah Round (11)
Sale Grammar School

The Fox

In my garden lives a fox he's red and white
He looks like a carrot with his long bushy tail
Like the leaves on the carrot.

He is sly and sneaky and he's like a snake
So small and slithering across the grass after his prey.

He smells and sniffs and snorts and pretends to taste
the taste in his mouth.
He hears the prey talking to one another
He leaps and lands right on his prey and swipes it in one
As he looks for anything watching him.

The trees were looking over him
And whispering in the wind as the grass was
swaying to and fro.

Hannah Wilson (11)
Sale Grammar School

Dad

This is about my dad, Pete,
He's got extremely smelly feet.
His favourite food he likes to eat,
Is tomato sauce on shredded wheat.

Apart from the fact that his shoes and socks pong,
My dad never does anything wrong.
He also likes to sing a song!
And while he does he rolls his tongue.

My dad's very, very kind,
Buying sweets, he doesn't mind.
Time for me he'll always find,
He's just super, in my mind.

Louise Mitchell (12)
Sale Grammar School

DETENTION

The guard's dark eyes are peering over at me
Why they are, is a mystery.
I can hear all those happy people outside
While I have been left so far behind.
I'm plotting really hard to find a way to leave
In here it's even hard to breathe.
Those intimidating eyes are watching me again
Trying to make me feel the pain
Of not handing my homework in
(Like *that's* some sort of terrible sin!)
Oh let me go, please set me free
You don't want a dreadful person like me!
I want to get out, I need to get out
But no one listens as I shout.
I've got to escape, I've got to find a way
If I want to see the light of another day.
So all you little kids out there
Hand in your homework
Or don't bother,
But beware!

Maxine Milner (11)
Sale Grammar School

ISOLATION

Waiting, wondering, waiting,
Cold, useless, helpless, trapped,
Isolated, lonely, heartbroken,
Like sending a fox to the hounds,
As hopeless as a dog washed up on the shore,
As weak and as weary as an old boot,
As angry and as mad as a trapped hyena,
Petrified, hurt, distant,
Shivering, perished, desolate, confined,
My eyes twinkling like the stars in the
Sky with fear in my eyes,
I long to breathe the air of freedom.

       Isolation.

Wesley Royle (12)
Sale Grammar School

THE FIREWORKS

The fireworks are like glitter
The fireworks swoosh up and down like a yo-yo.
They shoot up swish, swoosh and then tinkle down
like a waterfall.

Catherine wheels spin round and round like a car wheel,
The rockets bang, bang, bang, bang, deafening you.
The colours are the rainbow
The fireworks are like fiery flowers
Whizzing and shooting here and there.

The screamers, scream like a cat when you tread on its tail.
Rip, rap, crackle like Rice Krispies
And they're as hot as milk in an oven.

Natalie Goodier (12)
Sale Grammar School

A TRIP TO THE DENTIST

It's Friday afternoon
With fifteen minutes to go
Now I'm full of gloom
Instead of a happy glow.

I'm on my way
It doesn't take long
I wish it was a Saturday
Then I'd be singing a whole new song.

As we enter through the door
Walking past the room
I hear a man give such a roar
Knowing it's my turn soon!

I was asked to sit and wait
So I read a magazine
That was slightly out of date
Then I heard my name called 'Christine.'

Up I get
This is such a burden
In the seat I sit
Faced by the dental surgeon!

Full of fear
Feelings of woe
Drilling sound within the ear
Wishing it was time to go.

It's not me
And I'm so glad
It's my mum
And that's not too bad!

Laura Moran (11)
Sale Grammar School

ARNOLD

I have a pet called Arnold,
He loves to eat and play.
And when it is his bedtime,
He lies down in the hay.

I have a pet called Arnold,
His teeth are sharp and long.
But if you don't clean out his hutch,
It can smell rather strong!

I have a pet called Arnold,
He loves to run around.
But when it is a rainy day,
I'm afraid he is hutch-bound!

I have a pet called Arnold,
He's cleaned out twice a week.
If you don't give him treats each day,
Then you will hear him squeak.

I have a pet called Arnold,
He isn't very big.
His silky fur is black and brown,
He is a guinea pig.

Daniel Christopherson (11)
Sale Grammar School

THE TREE

A tree swings gracefully in the wind
Its branches look like skinny bony fingers
Reaching out to grab anyone it sees.

Its funny shaped skin takes flight in the winter
It looks deranged.
Its one scaly fat leg digs deep into
The ground for security.

Its big bones are high in the trees
Protected by its weird skin
Its long hands reach out and move when
The wind disturbs.

The funny shaped skin changes colour in the winter
It goes crispy and old then just falls
To the ground.

Michael Kershaw (11)
Sale Grammar School

SICK

I woke up one morning with a pain in my head,
The pain was piercing my skull like a knife.
I thought that I'd better stay in my bed,
I would have to miss school; what terrible strife!

I tried to get up to go to the loo,
My legs felt so heavy, as heavy as lead.
They just wouldn't move; were they stuck with glue?
But when I stood up I felt dizzy in the head.

My stomach was churning around and around,
So I went back to bed to have a lie down.
Now it was certain that I would be housebound,
But in came my mum; on her face was a frown.

'What's the matter with you, you terrible boy,
You're supposed to be down, getting ready for school?
School is fun, you will have great joy,
Don't lie here like a stubborn mule!'

But, my mum went to work and left me alone,
Here in my large house, all on my own!

Adam Christopherson (13)
Sale Grammar School

THE EXTREME SEASONS

The summer is golden and glistening,
Daisies are fresh on the lawn.
The dew in the morning sunlight,
Is gone by the afternoon.
People are lying on beaches,
On the grainy sand.
The tide is gradually coming in,
Bringing the shells in once more.

The winter is harsh and freezing,
And is drawing in once again.
The trees and streets are covered,
In cold, crisp, white snow.
Children are dressed in soft, warm clothes,
Scarves, gloves and hats.
Playing in the school playground,
Chucking snowballs about.

Holly Lawton (11)
Sale Grammar School

SICK

What is the meaning of sick?
Can the same word be used to describe
A child dying in a hospice bed
And a child, off-colour enjoying the attention
For some it brings pain and suffering.
For others a welcome break from school,
A mother's undivided attention
Warm drinks and phone calls from friends
One sick child brings devastation to a family,
Just a little inconvenience to another.

Recovery for some lasts just a day
Others will never achieve this.
The long struggle to health can be ever elusive
For these unfortunate children
They die
Next time you say you're sick, think what it really means.

Anna Cotton (13)
Sale Grammar School

THE SPIDER

So there we were, me staring at it
and it staring at me . . .

I was in my shed looking for my netball,
It was then that I saw it,
It was as big as a basketball . . .
Black as the night.
It ran at me
I screamed for Mummy and Daddy but no one heard,
I was hot, shaking - felt sick.
The walls were looking at me, laughing.
It was then when I saw the most wonderful thing.
It climbed to the top of the play box,
And started spinning the most beautiful web,
It was the first time I had ever watched a spider spin,
Then Mummy called me for dinner,
I said goodbye to my spider
And for the last time.
I looked at it and it looked at me.

Heather Edwards (12)
Sale Grammar School

SICK

It started with a temperature,
And then up came the rash,
Mum whisked me to the doctors,
In a moment and a flash.

'Well, well' said the doc,
'What have we here?'
He looked in my mouth,
And then in my ears.

'Oh dear' he remarked,
'Here what we have,
    is a case
you never have had.'

'What has she got?'
Asked my mum.
'Hold on' he said,
And then squeezed my thumb.

'Ouch' I squealed,
'What was that for?'
'I'm sorry' he replied,
'Will you walk through that door?'

'Soon you will notice
Some big red spots.
What you have is
Chickenpox!'

Amanda Graham (13)
Sale Grammar School

THE SEASIDE

The sea gently lapped against the rock,
Washing upon the sand.
But all too suddenly the sea can change
And hurtle onto land.
The children at the seaside build castles and moats too.
I like going to the seaside,
Do you?
The children find the shells that wash upon the shore,
When it's time to go home they always plead for more.
They run along the beach jumping in and out the spray,
They hoped it would never end on that hot blue May.
But the sea can be different - a dark and restless blue,
Far away from the children, the land, the dunes and flume.

Matthew Greenhalgh (11)
Sale Grammar School

GHOULISH

As I walked into the dull, grey castle, a shiver went up my spine.
The guide, who I didn't like the look of, shoved us inside.
First we walked down the dingy passageways
And we saw something even the ghostly guide couldn't describe.
Second by second it was getting darker.
Some people cried out and left, but us brave souls went on.
We briefly went into the Great Dining Room.
We visited the bedrooms for the lords and ladies of the land,
Kitchens and bathrooms we passed.
Then something happened that nobody expected
We saw . . . the slaves quarters and caught sight of the human remains
And a knife in someone's hand, possibly cooking, possibly murdering
one of the slaves.
We'll never know!

Peter Smithson (11)
Sale Grammar School

MY SCHOOL

My school is weird,
Totally different.
My school is stranger,
Than any of yours.

Our French teacher is Spanish,
Our Spanish teacher is French,
The English teacher can't spell,
She's totally weird as well.

Whenever we have science,
We hide underneath the desks.
Because our science teacher,
Is a mad scientist!

Our geography teacher can't read maps,
Our geography teacher always gets lost.
Our geography teacher can't tell
Wales from Wrexham.

My head teacher is a film star,
He starred in Goldeneye!
All the pupils go wild in assembly,
But he was still the bad guy.

As you see my school is weird,
You would be weird to disagree!
But the weirdest teacher is the games teacher,
He's in a bobsleigh team.

Jill Thomason (11)
Sale Grammar School

I WISH I WAS DEAD

The screams of pain are in my head,
I cannot escape them,
My heart is pounding,
My body is trembling,
My leg is broken from the guards beating me,
I cannot deny my true hope in here,
It is to be killed very soon,
I am always in pain so I might as well go,
Here come the guards marching along,
They usually take people away,
They never return,
Who will they pick, I hope it is me,
They are looking at me now and talking so quietly,
I know what they will be thinking
Yes, I was right, they are leading me away,
To a vast open space,
They have left me in the middle,
With soldiers around me,
They all have rifles,
I know what is coming,
I have been waiting for it,
Soon I will go ever so slow,
The bang of the guns has punctured my body,
As I lie on the floor,
I can hear some dogs coming,
And a gentle smile rolls across my face.

Andrew Lugsden (13)
Sale Grammar School

IN THE AFTERNOON

In the afternoon lots of things go on,
You do your homework,
You have your tea,
You go to the toilet,
And then you watch TV,
Nice and refreshed you feel,
You go out and play
With your friends,
And people start to pray
I stay out and bat watch,
In the beautiful sunset,
Red, orange, yellow and blue
And I play with my pet,
My brother comes and annoys me,
And we do a bet,
That United will beat Liverpool
I win, I win shout out I,
I clean my teeth,
And in my bed I lie.

Mark Collier (11)
Sale Grammar School

SICK

I woke up one morning at 8 o'clock,
To find that I was covered all over in spots.
I went downstairs to tell my mummy,
She checked on my arms,
And checked on my tummy.
The spots grew itchy,
The spots turned red.
Mummy phoned the doctor,
Then sent me to bed.

The appointment we had was at 1.29
So off we went within plenty of time.
We waited with patience till the buzzer went,
Then went in the room and said 'Hello Doctor Bent
As you can see, Laura's covered in spots.
And am I right in saying, it's the chickenpox?'
The doctor said I should buy a tube of calamine,
And in a few days I would feel 'Just fine!'

Laura Hughes (13)
Sale Grammar School

SICK

They say I've got the flu,
I know this can't be true.
They've sent me up to bed,
My nose is bright, bright red.
It's probably from all the blowing of my nose,
For some reason I'm aching from head to toes.
I don't know how this can be,
But why is it happening to me?
I feel all rotten inside,
I want to go under the covers and hide.
How can I feel so bad?
It's making me all so mad.
I think I'm going to be sick. Oh no!
Where's a sink? I've got to go.

I'm now feeling more unwell,
Will I survive, only time will tell.

Lisa Kelly (13)
Sale Grammar School

STUCK!

Here I am, stuck in a room,
It's rusty, old
Quite a dump too!
The ceiling's mouldy.
The walls are damp.
The floor has woodworm.
The dust,
Well it's making me cough like mad!
There's an ant farm in the corner.
Crisp packets are covering the floor.
I'm not well,
I feel claustrophobic,
I'm going mad!
My friend's locked me in here,
Saying we are going to play hide and seek.
I was on, of course!
They ran out the room and bolted the door!
I don't know where I am,
But I know this, as they let me out,
I'm starting a war between them and me,
They will see!
What's this? They are letting me out!
I run out the door,
As fast as I can,
I lock them in,
That will show them!

Charlotte Kay (11)
Sale Grammar School

ISOLATED

Like a terrified ox
I am isolated.
Listening to my heart pounding,
Stiff through coldness and fear.
I can see nothing,
It is as black as a moonless sky.
I can taste the hunger . . .
The fear.

I am as hungry as an unfed lion,
As thirsty as a man,
Walking in the scorching heat.
I'm as helpful as a
Sword with no blade,
A key with no lock.
Heartbreaking pain makes me
Shiver and shake.

I feel as terrorised as a
Captured dolphin,
A leaf in a violent storm.
As intimidated as a
Bullied child,
With nowhere to run.
As lost as a pea in a
Soup for 10,000.
Isolated.
That's what I am.
Isolated.

Rachael Morris (12)
Sale Grammar School

ALL ALONE

I'm all alone
Nobody needs me, nobody wants me
No family, no friends

I work all day to raise my lodgings
Climbing up chimneys
Inhaling dirty black soot
It's so dark, so stuffy

When I don't raise enough money for my lodgings
The vile landlord lets me sleep in the street
It's so cold, the wind knocks me over
The rain forms damp puddles around my weary body
I can smell the coal from my landlord's room,
It's ever so warm,
I can almost feel the soft, blanket of his bed covering me in safety.

But then the spine-chilling wind blows on my neck,
That's when I realise, I'm all alone.

Andrew Blake (11)
Sale Grammar School

MISERY

There she stands with worry and depression,
The thought of sadness looming over her,
The family has been torn apart like a piece of paper,
Her bag clung to her side and her doll tucked neatly in her hand.

The word misery was stuck in her head
Like chewing gum to a school desk,
Her palms sweaty and her eyes red and sore from crying.
The pain in her heart was not fading,
Misery misery misery misery . . .

The word misery rang in her head like a bell,
This word would be with her until she was reunited
With her family,
She picked up her satchel ready to board the plane
With her doll still tucked under her arm,
She took one positive breath and several negative steps
To *misery*.

Haley Beckford (13)
Sale Grammar School

MY MISCHIEVOUS PUPPY

'Run, run get out of the way,
She is after your shoelace she wants you to play.'
She will chase after anything human or ball.
She will jump over flowerbeds and climb over walls.
When she comes in with mud on her nose,
She doesn't think of washing, but wipes it on your clothes!
You can't let our puppy go out of your sight,
Because when you look around later you might have a fright.
She'll have taken your knickers and chewed them to bits.
She'll have raided the cupboards and eaten our Weetabix.
Her jewel-like eyes are bold and bright,
Her soft clean fur is black and white
When she has been bad we put her in bed,
She will sit up straight and tilt her head,
She'll look at us sadly all puzzled and confused.
The process starts again: 'Watch out for your shoes!'

Alex Rhind (12)
Sale Grammar School

TRAPPED WITH EMOTIONS

The young boys and girls watch the freedom
The others have.
They stare at each other and sympathise.
Consecutive screams are all they hear.
They reach out to each other to keep
Themselves sane.
They clench their fists, and force the anger
Away.
Fences everywhere, nowhere to escape.
Maybe someday they will awake.
A life is all they hope for,
And their own beliefs.
So they don't have to
Live with all this deceit.
Survival is a question they cannot answer,
But death is a question maybe they can
Answer.
Death.
Survival.
Who knows?

Dean Fletcher (13)
Sale Grammar School

MY CAT BONNIE

With fur as black as a raven's wing,
And eyes of emerald-green,
He sits so proud upon my knee,
Silent and serene.

There's nowhere that is out of bounds,
To one as lithe as he,
He can scale a six foot garden fence,
And climb the tallest tree,

He's very fussy with his food,
And cat food's not for him,
He likes roast chicken and roast ham,
And salmon with no skin.

He sleeps upon my bed at night,
Across my legs and feet,
I never like to wake him up,
Because he looks so sweet.

Hannah Cordiner (11)
Sale Grammar School

ISOLATION

Abandoned, lost, forgotten.
Trapped, desolate, worthless.
Longing for love like a lost orphan child,
Knowing I'll die makes my imagination run wild.
Everyone I see, I think they want to kill me.
Even the kind old man on the corner seems to have my key to death.

I want to die,
And I have no tears left to cry.
I can taste death in the air.
No matter where I turn,
I can see death's dark blanket before me.

Trapped, alone, useless.
Isolated with nowhere to run.
Abandoned,
Lost,
Forgotten.

Lisa Moore (13)
Sale Grammar School

THE CURRY

In the room
The Balti dish sits
People sit talking and sharing
The curry.

It's hot and spicy
Naan bread and poppadums.
People passing round and sharing
The curry.

It smells really good
I've not got any.
People eating and sharing
The curry.

'Would you like some?'
I say 'Yes please'
Now me and people sharing
The curry.

Now it's gone
There's no more left
People order some more and share
The curry!

Emily Hallett (12)
Sale Grammar School

LOOK OUT OF THE WINDOW

As I peep through a pane of glass
I can see many things.
The leaves on trees
And the buzzing bees,
Just swaying and buzzing to and fro.

As I gaze through a window
I can see lots of things,
The red bricks
And the brown sticks,
Just sitting there on the ground.

Ben Wiltshire (11)
Sale Grammar School

THE GAME

You think a game is just a
game where the taking part
counts. That is as in most
games where it is just luck,
you win you lose, it's all
the same but
not in this game.
In this game
you are playing
for
life
you
lose you die. In
this game you
land on places
and things on the roll of a
dice. If you land on a
graveyard you go to your grave.
If you win you are lucky or
a very good fighter, if you lose,
sorry, better luck in your second
life. Ha, ha, ha.

Adam Fenton (11)
Sale Grammar School

THE TRIAL PACK OF NESCAFÉ

All I did was open the door,
And there it was on
                    the
                         step.
Just sitting there on the floor,
Was the trial pack of Nescafé.

I put the kettle on to boil,
And waited for the switch to flip
I got out my favourite mug,
And then took the first sip.

Dark bubbles popping on top,
The mug warming my hand.
Smooth texture filling my mouth,
The taste from another land.

Sarah Stead (11)
Sale Grammar School

STAIRCASES

The swirling staircase,
Where does it take us?
Where will we go?
Will it ever stop, down the deep black hole?
I hope that we will stop soon,
I'm feeling rather dizzy,
This must be what it feels like,
In a drink that's fizzy.
The staircase in my house is very boring,
I walk up and down it all day,
And then at night I end up snoring.

Jayne Marlow (11)
Sale Grammar School

MICROSCOPIC ANIMALS

Bacteria, now there's a thought
Can make up to the biggest wart
They multiply by the hour
Giving them lots of power

Amoeba, now there's a story
Moving round just like a Tory
They devour things like a mob
Leaving the remains (a lifeless blob)

Viruses, just wait a sec
Are really a big pain in the neck
They make people really ill
And they aren't a very big thrill.

Daniel Connor (11)
Sale Grammar School

ANGELICA

Angelica is a girl,
But not an ordinary girl.
She's bossy, naughty, bratty and mean,
But she always gets away with things.

She likes cookies and biscuits,
Every time her mum buys cookies they're gone in two minutes.
She steals toys and teddy bears,
But she always gets away with things.

Her mum caught her one time,
Stealing a Barbie doll.
She got grounded for two months,
She didn't get away with this thing!

Adam Robson (12)
Sale Grammar School

MY DREAM

I dreamt about a movie star,
Looking down on the crowd below,
flicking her hair to and fro.
She stared at me I thought what's wrong?
I suddenly felt weak not strong,
My face was going redder and redder
What should I do?
Then I suddenly felt better.
My mum was there saying,
        What's wrong my dear?
        But then I screamed
        Madonna's staring at *me!*

Fiona Drysdale (11)
Sale Grammar School

MY AUNT

My aunt lives in London
She works at the BBC
She lives in a flat
But pretends it's by the sea

My aunt rides a bicycle to work
It goes clank, clank all the time
She also pretends she's
        Shakespeare
I wish she would just mime.

My aunt wears odd socks every day
And they are very smelly
She never wears platform shoes
So she always wears wellies.

My aunt invites people round for
                dinner.
But she always cooks chilli
She makes it really, really spicy
And she almost killed Billy.

Kate Howorth (11)
Sale Grammar School

NAZI

Death
Decay
Emptiness
Trapped in the cold heartless
Hands of the Nazis
We lay in death
Yet still suffering
Bones are all that are left.
That and the feelings of disturbed souls.
Humiliation still sounds in the drone of bulldozers.
Escape was once death
Now death has become decay.
My only comfort is in a commune
with my friend, my family and a Nazi.

Lianne Ramsden (13)
Sale Grammar School

COLD HEARTS

Isolated
nowhere to go, nothing
trapped, confined, helpless
I am a helpless prey
I am being destroyed by my own fear
lost, lonely
lying to myself
Saying to myself I will get through it
Horrified, shivering, shaking
dark, murky, black
waiting for death
A prisoner of my own fear
Isolated!

Christopher Smith (12)
Sale Grammar School

ISOLATION

Isolated but fearless
Hungry, weary and restless,
But never petrified.
Sat staring into an endless circle of dots,
As lifeless as a rock, six feet under.
As lost as one carrot in a stew for 10,000.

For me, life does not exist as a destiny,
But as a bottomless free fall roller-coaster,
Racing out of control.
The only thing I fear is the chamber of hell,
The only thing I wish is that no one grieves my death.

I am still alive physically, but my soul died long ago,
Like a burning candle, I face the end,
Isolated but fearless.

Claire Brownlee (13)
Sale Grammar School

ISOLATION

I'm isolated on this cold winter night,
Shivering, frightened and alone.
Watching and listening for any movement,
Speeding over the waters like an E-15 fighter plane.
My eyes are like shining pieces of gold,
People rushing around like panicking animals.
I've been waiting and waiting for hours,
I am scared, hungry and getting stiff,
I'm isolated and I will be for a long time.

Christopher Dunn (12)
Sale Grammar School

DOWN BEHIND THE DUSTBIN

Down behind the dustbin
I met a dog called Fred
'What are you looking for?' I asked
'I'm looking for some bread!'

Down behind the dustbin
I met a dog called Pat
'Hello there' she said
'Do you like my pink fluffy hat?'

Down behind the dustbin
I met a dog called Dee
'Ouch!' she roared
'I've been stung by a bee!'

Brian Crockett (11)
Sale Grammar School

WAR IS . . .

War is the fear in your eyes of tomorrow.
War is death, loss and sorrow.
War is a tear shed for the loss of each life.
War is the deadly harsh cut of a knife.
War is greed in the heart of the power.
War is the colour of a blood-red flower.
War is the taste of the thickening smoke,
Choking you at the back of your throat.
War is the sound of sirens warning.
War is the fear of the new day's dawning.
War is the screams of the children lost in the fight.
War - an everlasting night.

Lottie Galloway (12)
Sale Grammar School

ISOLATION

All alone,
Sat in deathly silence, isolated
from all humanity,
I have overwhelming feelings
of emptiness and fear,
Hoping and praying I close my eyes,
And imagine what it is to be free,
As free as an eagle,
Swooping low around the steepest of cliffs,
While the fierce waves pound
against the rocks below.

I am contained in a small
contaminated cell,
As I look around, shivers
are sent up my spine,
I feel numb at the thought of
spending the rest of my living days here.

The horrific odour of dank,
neglected conditions has
combined with the air,
Its musty smell fills my lungs
like a dense poisoned gas.

An unrelenting tide of sewer rats
invade my space,
My bed of warm straw is now
a home for flea-infested rats.

I would bend down on my knees
for a way to escape this tragic torture.
But for now I must stay with
the rodents and their own filth.
With hatred in the back of my throat,
It will only stop if I escape
But it is more likely that I will die.

Rebecca Gunning (12)
Sale Grammar School

SICK

Sick, the pain throbbing in my head,
Repeating its painful song over and over again,
When will it stop?

Sick, the endless hours of being miserable,
Lying, wishing to be well, not again,
Your thoughts of better times bring you through.

Sick, the cramp of an empty stomach,
The weakness caused by flu,
And the heat of a fever, changing to cold.

Sick, the medicines and remedies,
That taste disgusting and strong,
But it's better them than being sick.

Sick, the things you're missing, being with your friends,
The work you will have to catch up on,
But worrying will make you feel worse.

Sick, the fever is loosening its grip,
The pleasure of being well again, no more pain,
Against the annoyance of returning to school,
I hate being sick.

Laurence Byrne (13)
Sale Grammar School

THE WORM

Johnny thought I wouldn't do it,
he said I'd be afraid.
I told him that I'd prove it,
then the bet was made.
Kids gathered from every corner,
to watch me writhe and squirm.
At the tip of my middle finger,
sat a grand and bloated worm.
The whispered hush of the audience,
turned rowdy and chaos broke out.
I could just about hear the words of the cheers,
and the chants they began to shout.
The sticky ooze left behind by the worm,
made me cringe with utter disgust.
But I had to let the worm carry on,
I must, I must, I must!
As the worm approached my elbow,
the commotion slowly died down.
Intent gazes were fixed on me,
but Johnny's face held a frown.
The worm began to linger,
it dawdled for a time.
But it gradually inched forward,
and crossed the finishing line.
A cheer went up from the sidelines,
and Johnny began to whine.
He handed over the shiny gold coin,
the victory was all mine.
I stood and basked in the glory,
but a rumbling echo inside,
silenced the din from my friends,
and their anxious eyes opened wide

They watched my face go green,
I had to grab something quick.
There was poor Johnny's lunch box
Oh dear! I was going . . . to be sick

Samantha Daley (13)
Sale Grammar School

THE FOOTBALL MATCH

The chatter of the boys getting changed
Thud, clatter, bang.
Out of the changing room
Slam the door
Tramping of feet
Clatter of boots
Squelching through the mud
Troop into positions
Wait for the shriek
Of the referee's whistle
The thud of the ball echoes all around
A darting run a swaying run
From the right winger
A crunching tackle
The rumble of the crowd
The stopwatch ticking to full time
The last thumping kick of the ball
Screaming into the rippling net
1-0 to Sale Grammar.

Robert McKie (11)
Sale Grammar School

ISOLATION

Isolation
Filled with despondent anguish
Disarranged and separated from the freedom of the world.
Helpless and wasting away
As dejected as a young child
Like a brittle twig in a storm out at sea
As dejected as a young child
Helpless and wasting away
Disarranged and separated from the freedom of the world.
Filled with despondent anguish
Isolation

Jennifer Midwinter (12)
Sale Grammar School

ISOLATION

Isolation,
Watching, waiting,
Frightened and robbed of my life,
As terrified as a hunted fox,
I have the rushing roar of terror inside me,
I hear prisoners groaning and moaning,
I hear coughing, crying and coldness,
As fearful as a wild bird trapped in a cage,
Like a fly caught in a spider's web,
Desolate and deserted,
Shivering and shaking,
Isolation.

Elisabeth Speakman (12)
Sale Grammar School

DEATH CAMP

I was caught two weeks ago often being chased, like a fish
being chased by sharks.
I'm living in conditions fit for a pig, a stench like mouldy vegetables.
My bed is the right size for a tiny baby,
some of the people around me are dead.
All the people living here are sick,
they have deadly diseases and there's no help for them.
Any people that still have their energy are sent to the fields
to do labour in the wind, rain and snow.
I feel like a child cornered by a gang of murderous bullies.
There's no way anyone can survive more than a couple of weeks here.
I can't understand it, herds of people go into the showers every day
and I've never seen any of them come back out.
We are matchsticks, there's no way out of here.

Tadek Gwiazdowski-Bzdega
Sale Grammar School

ISOLATED

I am isolated,
Shivering, confused, alone in deathly silence.
I feel bewildered, hated, no strength to carry on,
A speck of dust on a poor man's coat.
Crushed, like an injured tiger cooped up in a cage,
Desperately praying to be removed from this shadow of death.
A sharp dagger of fear plunges through my heart,
I dream of freedom, to run like an antelope,
Away from this crisis.
Deep down in my heart I know I will
Never be removed from uncertainty.
Forlorn, separated, lonesome
Forever . . . isolated.

Lauren Armson (12)
Sale Grammar School

FISHY TAILS

I am a fish
        who swims in the sea
I eat with the jellyfish but the
        sharks eat me!

Inside a shark's belly
        it's really dark
Behind the ribcage is where
        I'll park!

A nice little spot is where
        I've found
Nobody can move me,
        not even for a pound.

Hey wait a minute
        I've been offered more
£1.50! What galore.

Laura Mullen (11)
Sale Grammar School

IRAQ

Smell the smell of the desert sand,
See the sight of the tigress,
Eat the food of heaven,
And see the sight of the city.

See the people all with smiles,
Offering you all they have,
The lovely, beautiful, pleasant, heavenly,
Unappreciated Iraq.

It's beautiful, it's hot,
It's full of sights to see.
The people who have been to Iraq,
Have all come back in glee.

When you have been to Iraq,
Your life seems to change.
You love the country with all its might,
When you have seen the lovely light shown
By the lovely Iraq.

Hazem Fahad (11)
Sale Grammar School

WINTER DAYS

As I sit on the window sill,
By the heat of the freshly laid fire,
I gaze into the lamp-lit street,
Not a soul around,
No one to make me smile,
No one to make me forget the drab winter.
I start to dream,
Dream of the spring,
Dream of the flowers and birds to come,
Then I drift back to reality,
And realise I have to sit through the winter first,
I have to sit alone and freeze,
When the fire runs out,
No one cares,
No one is worried
What if the spring never comes,
What if we're living in winter forever,
What if the flowers never wake,
Could you imagine living in winter forever?

Jenna Thornton (13)
Sale Grammar School

A Sight To Behold

Looking down on the earth I see,
All its natural beauty,
Fields of green, oceans of blue
trees of great height and bright flowers too.

I see wild animals of all kinds,
from the fierce great tigers to the race of mankind
Different countries from Africa to Spain,
Different languages, nobody is the same.

But then I look closer
And tell me why I see,
Wars and arguments
How could this be?

People abusing and destroying the earth,
Cutting down trees
And much,
much worse.

The world with its wonders.
What a breathtaking place,
So why do some people,
Put it to waste?

Stacey Ashe (13)
Sale Grammar School

Fluttering In The Wind

As I sleep I catch the flight of birds,
who ride the autumn breeze.

No clouds, no dust, no smoke.

I see the wind gently lifting their feathers,
feathers worn from endless flight.
With effortless ease they glide, this invisible force.
So silent, so peaceful, their journey continues.

If you too can see this scene, then you can see my dreams.

Sean Pritchard (12)
Sale Grammar School

LEAVING PRIMARY SCHOOL

'Hello!' we said some years ago,
'Goodbye,' we're saying now.
No more teachers, hallelujah!
Telling us why or how.

No more lumpy custard,
looking like cement.
No offence, dinner ladies,
but you know what I meant.

No more long assemblies,
sitting cross-legged on the floor.
I'm glad somebody woke me up,
I think I was going to snore.

No more singing silly songs,
with which we don't agree,
I wish I'd brought my Walkman,
and a decent tape with me.

No more headmaster,
and the teaching staff.
On behalf of all Year 6,
Thanks, it's been a laugh.

Nicola Griffiths (12)
Sale Grammar School

MY ISOLATION

Alone,
Alone, annoyed and petrified at the frustrating situation,
Cursing and kicking at the walls that have confined
me in this domain of darkness.
Trapped like a fly in the spider's web of doom,
My mind as dull as a rainy winter's day,
The darkness is spread as if a black sheet
has fallen on the skies,
I am an ant under a human's foot.

Silence,
Silence, paranoia, and agony pass through my mind,
The thought of death makes me shiver
like a baby in the icy cold water of a pond,
I feel as if a giant is resting on my shoulder.
The eyes of rats come to me like flashing lights
through the dull soot.
It seems like death is to be my destiny.
The blood on my face feels like 1000 painful deaths.

Mark Cornthwaite (12)
Sale Grammar School

GETTING OUT

Poor child!
She is a sad terrified little girl
Watching
Waiting for her future to be told
She is like a frightened rabbit
Desperate to get out.
Desperate to go home to her family
Clutching, tightly to her precious belongings
Trying so desperately not to cry
Wondering in fear
Who will take her home.

She is all alone except for her doll
So young
So healthy
So innocent
As she boards the ship
Not knowing if she'll come back
Not knowing if she'll survive
Not knowing if she'll see her
Family again
Not knowing, just not knowing . . .

Sophie Roberts (13)
Sale Grammar School

ISOLATION

I was alone in
a dark dull room.
Alone as a man
in a jungle.
Petrified as a
hunted animal.
Waiting, waiting
Waiting for my
end to come.
I see the dark
shadow of death
hanging over my head.
The feel of being alone
stabs me in the back
and creates my
apocalypse.

Sean Modder (12)
Sale Grammar School

WOMEN'S WAR

Team spirit,
That's the key,
Colourful banners and cups of tea,
Mend and make do,
Waste not want not,
Saving money in a pot!

In the factories, on the camps,
Cheerily, cheerily keeping the country.

But behind the banners, the bands and parades,
Lies a lonely woman,
Left in the dark,
Not knowing if she will see her sweetheart.

Graham Cook (13)
Sale Grammar School

THE CITY

Hustling, bustling in the city,
Dirty, dark clouds blocking out the sun
People shouting to their children
Trees and bushes there are none.

In the centre of the city,
Shops and office blocks reaching for the sky,
The air so very hot and misty
Stores with upper floors up so high.

Nothing you can do about the pollution in the city
Evil dark shadows with no light.
How can we stop it no one knows
Nobody can help our fight.

Sam Gaunt (11)
Sale Grammar School

YOUR ISOLATION

Trapped as a prisoner,
The key thrown away,
You didn't plan this,
You didn't mean to get caught,
The judge was on their side,
Your solicitor was no good,
10 years in jail,
Just for not paying for food.
For trying to survive the winter,
Only 9 years 11 months left of your life,
At least you didn't get the chop.
Trapped like a lion's meal,
When the lion has been starved,
A prisoner of winter.

Stephen Eaton (12)
Sale Grammar School

MEETING FEAR ITSELF

Here I am alone with fear!
It's the only thing that can get me.
So I have to be quick running away from my fear,
the monster that lurks inside me!

I am not as wise as an owl when I'm thinking.
I'm as confused as a deserted baby!
It's a terrible place and I must escape from
my own damp, dark thought!

Paranoid and petrified am I, of the fear
(I cannot describe)
I must escape before it's too late.
or never again will I thrive!

Ceryn Coughlin (12)
Sale Grammar School

THE WOOD

Isolated,
Trapped in endless freedom,
Thought I wanted to live a little but now it's running,
hiding, watching and waiting.
Isolated, alone and forsaken,
Like an injured lion cast away by his pride,
But also like a so small a fish in a vast and deep sea,
dark freezing and annoyed,
In a few hours I'll be sleeping, worrying and hoping.
Trapped in the endless barrier of freedom
Isolated!

Michael Stoddart (12)
Sale Grammar School

MY ISOLATION

Helpless
Speechless and shocked
Trapped
Frightened
My mind was a leaf being blown away
in an autumn day.
I was as useless as a merciless slave
I could hear the Jews who were
waiting to be executed crying and weeping.

Shivering
thinking
dreaming.

Walking through the Sahara Desert
without any water.
Like a deer being chased
by a gang of cheetahs.
I was a man stuck
in a glass mirror maze.
I was as weak as an injured ox.
Watching
staring
glancing
I felt disabled.

Yousif Al-Tamimy (12)
Sale Grammar School

I DIDN'T MEAN TO!

I didn't mean to drop my drink,
Or put the goldfish in the sink.

I didn't mean to push my cousin,
Or put Playdoh in the oven.

I didn't mean to wet the dog,
Or push my sister in the bog.

I didn't mean to kick the cat,
Or ruin grandma's favourite hat.

I didn't mean to lose my key,
Or scare that cat up the tree.

I didn't mean to eat that pie,
Or poke my friend in the eye.

It was one accident after another,
Sorry, sorry, sorry, Mother!

Lauren Garner (13)
Sale Grammar School

PREY CATCHERS

The racing car is a cheetah waiting for his food.
He starts his engine ready to go
But the cheetah's enemy does not know.
Beep! The buzzer has gone, the cheetah has started.
The enemy has noticed that he is coming up behind him,
As fast as a dolphin not swimming slowly,
The cheetah's still running,
The car is still driving
The car is still in first place
The cheetah is still behind his enemy.

Boom! The cheetah's food has been caught,
He is enjoying his meal, a black and white zebra,
And the rest are watchers staring at the cheetah's mouth
digging into its body.

The car has come first, he has won his medal,
And all that can be done is to
Rest In Peace.

Troy Williams-Condor (11)
Sale Grammar School

FROZEN

Squashed, enclosed like a transported animal
as I stare forward I see
only darkness.

I was as freezing as
Jack Frost in winter, nipping
at my toes and fingers.
The ice had clamped me
like a piece of wood just
waiting to be crushed,
crushed like an ant underfoot.

As I hear the ice break
I think of McCoy's cheese
and chive potato chips being
crunched and consumed
in a man's large mouth.
The sound streaks down
my spine as the walls get
closer and closer.

If I could only reach out
and touch a warm hand.

Jack Egan (12)
Sale Grammar School

THE SEA

I once went swimming in the salty sea,
To see all the spectacular sea creatures,
I saw some small silvery fish and they twinkled like stars,
In the clear, shimmering water.

I stood up and looked down, the sun's reflection shone into my eyes,
I felt the soft, squelchy sand sliding through my toes and
The stones sticking into my feet.

The salty taste of the sea stayed in my mouth,
The shrieks of the seagulls sounded like the screams of a child,
I made my way towards the shore, the sound of swishing
Water followed behind me.
The stones and the soft sand were warmed by the sun,
I lay down to rest in the sun with the cool sea water
Rolling and crashing over my feet.

Natalie Silcock (11)
Sale Grammar School

LION

The lion stalks its prey through
the long dry grass of the plain,
like an assassin
it crouches low like a coiled spring
and growls very quietly like a kitten purring.

Then it explodes from its hiding place
like a bullet from a gun,
and they come face to face,
the prey shakes with fear like
a bird in the icy cold wind.

Then it sets off a chase
round and round they go like a tiger
trying to catch its own tail.

The lion manages to floor its prey
like a hammer hitting a nail.
It flicks out its razor-sharp claws
and in one big swipe the
prey is dead!

Nikki Williamson (11)
Sale Grammar School

NIGHT LIFE

The lights are dim the tables set,
It's where the in crowd have always met,
Knives and forks in pristine condition,
For every plate they know their mission.

The mood is romantic, the music slow,
The dance floor reflects the moonlit glow.
The waiters swarm in smartest suits,
Bearing cheese and biscuits and exquisite fruits.

The drinks are poured the bill shared,
It's Saturday night no expense spared.
Let's party, party, party, the night is young,
It's disco time and there are songs to be sung.

Christopher Buckley (13)
Sale Grammar School

IF I WERE A MILLIONAIRE

If I were a millionaire
I'd have lots of cash in my pocket.
Everyone would be so surprised
Their eyes would come out of their sockets!

If I were a millionaire
I'd buy everything.
I'd buy my dad a brand new car,
And buy my mum a diamond ring.

If I were a millionaire
I'd buy myself a tropical island,
I'd go swimming every day
And sunbathe on the sand.

If I were a millionaire
I'd wear the fanciest clothes.
I'd be covered in gold
Even on my nose.

If I were a millionaire
Everyone would stare.
I'd be so popular
If I were a millionaire.

Vicki Wiles (13)
Sale Grammar School

ISOLATION

I'm sitting here all alone,
Nowhere to go,
Nowhere to hide.
I yearn to be free,
Free as a bird,
I could fly and swoop,
Feel the wind in my face.
But no!
Not in here,
Four solid stone walls,
You can almost see the frost at first light.

It is like a room full of ice blocks,
I haven't felt my fingers for two whole days,
I sit and think,
An archaeologist will find me,
Preserved in an ice block
Many years from now.
I hear no other people,
Just a deathly silence,
A silence only heard by you,
It makes you shiver in your bones.
I'm lost in a world forgotten forever,
With nowhere to go and,
Nowhere to hide.

Heather Covell (12)
Sale Grammar School

WHAT I LIKE

I like to eat a sour apple,
which tingles my tongue as I crunch.

I like to smell fresh coffee,
as it bubbles away delightfully.

I love to touch a badger, so soft,
at the break of day in a moonlit sky.

I love to see the colourful sunset,
as the blazing sun moves slowly down, down, down.

I also like to see a Yorkshire pudding
rise like a pot being built up on a pottery machine.

Robert Wood (11)
Sale Grammar School

THE ONOMATOPOEIA STORM

Pitter, patter, drip, drop,
Pitter, patter, drip, drop,
Goes the cold, wet rain hitting the window,
As I sit warm and dry and cosy inside,
Watching the water trickle down the glass.

Bang, thump, crash, flash,
Bang, thump, crash, flash,
Goes the thunder and lightning brightening up the sky,
As I sit quietly and thoughtfully inside,
Watching people scurry by, trying to find shelter.

Whistle, whoosh, rustle, swoosh,
Whistle, whoosh, rustle, swoosh,
Goes the fierce harsh wind forcefully throwing the leaves,
As I sit peacefully and calmly inside,
Watching the helpless leaves brush past my window.

Another typical summer's day in Manchester.

Ella Dore (11)
Sale Grammar School

OUTRAGED AND ALONE

Helpless, feeble and weak,
Cramped,
Restless, living in hope,
Feeling hatred and pain.

He's seen the resentment in my eyes,
Fearing, yearning, waiting for freedom,
I cry for freedom,
I'd die for freedom,
I pray for freedom,
Freedom . . .

The twisting taunting screams of death,
Black windows, dark skies,
Clouds of dirty grey smoke.

Feeling hatred and pain,
Restless, living in hope,
Cramped,
Helpless, feeble and weak.

Kayleigh Baxter (12)
Sale Grammar School

A DAILY SCHOOL RECIPE

Take half a dozen teachers,
Shouting 'Sit down!'
And add 1,200 pupils jam-packed in corridors.
You also have to have a pinch of loud school bells,
So when it rings, there is silence no more!

Add a pinch of banging lockers, and a pinch of work.
In the classroom you will hear,
The scratching of the blackboard,
And the scratching of the chairs.

In the art block you will find,
All the work in a bubbling stew.
When you are trying to fish out your pen,
The steaming hot bells ring.

A hint of emptiness in the corridors,
Will finish off your cooking.
So hurry, hurry, hurry,
Off home you must go.
Come on don't just stand there,
Everyone else has gone,
So why don't you go too?

Stephanie Hodgkiss (11)
Sale Grammar School

THE SEASIDE DONKEY

Why do I have to be
a donkey trotting by the sea?

Why do I always have
little children sitting on me?

Why does that blazing sun
keep beating down on me?

Why can't I be in the shade
of a great big handsome tree?

Why are people paying to sit on top of me,
Instead of leaving me to roam the fields free?

Kerry Robson (13)
Sale Grammar School

ALONE

All on her own she stands so still
Clutching her things and her doll until
Someone comes and takes her away.
All she can think is where she'll be next day.
Standing like a soldier so straight and tall
Her face is so plain though, she feels like she'll fall.
Her battered coat and worn out shoes
Where are her family? She's waiting for news.
All the silent space in the deserted room.
All she is wishing for now is the time 'til her doom.
One small bag for all her things
Waiting for anyone, anything.

Janine Blackburn (13)
Sale Grammar School

FOOTBALL

The other team had the ball,
I was watching him like a lion watching its prey.
I then started running,
I was as fast as an ant tied to a rocket.
I took the ball like an owl swooping down to catch its prey.

I got the ball,
And I was running up the wing
I was dodging like a deer being chased by a lion.
It was getting closer,
I could feel it breathing down my neck.
And as I was about to shoot,
It went for the kill!

I was running in the box,
And I was tripped up.
I fell like a sack of potatoes.
I got a penalty,
I stepped up for it.
I ran as fast as a tortoise on a cheetah's back,
I kicked it as hard as Prince Naseem's punch,
It went in the back of the net.

Goal!

Mark James Flood (12)
Sale Grammar School

I'M A TREE

I'm writing a poem
About a tree
An oak or acorn
Which suits me?

Should I be big?
Should I be small?
Should I be stout
Or lean and tall?

I'm like a willow
Wispy long hair
Oh, like you're bothered!
In fact, why should you care?

Mbabazi Anita Turya (11)
Sale Grammar School

THE TIGER

The tall green luscious grass vibrates like taut violin strings
being plucked.
The dark shadowy silhouette envelops the stillness of the day.
As a murderer creeping with death in his heart.
His yellow eyes pierce and stare
As they cut their way through the curtains of the jungle.
Searching like a hungry hunter waiting to ensnare its prey.
His rising heartbeat quickens like the beat of a drum.
All its senses are tense and alert.
Like a sentry on night duty
With a twitch of his whiskers and a flick of his ears
He crouches like a weary old man
Licking his lips in eager anticipation.
A young gazelle glides into sight
Like a welcome ship on a hungry horizon.
With a sudden leap and gnashing of teeth
Gleaming like shining daggers
Clawing their way mercilessly into the innocent victim
The conquering camouflaged tiger
Has made his entrance on life's stage.
Cleverly like a well rehearsed actor
While the poor gazelle gasps and exits
His light is extinguished forever.

Lucy O'Gara (11)
Sale Grammar School

THE NEGLECTED PONY

It's hard to remember now,
What Bertie looked like when I first saw him.
He was as thin as a piece of wire,
His ribs were like a toast rack,
And his legs looked like muddy twigs,
The wounds all over his body were as red as tomatoes,
His mane was tangled, like vines crawling up a tree,
And his eyes were as gloomy as the fog.

It took months to put everything right,
But soon his eyes shone bright,
Bright as the stars,
His legs started to become sturdy little things,
And the wounds all over his body were gone at the speed of light.

Now he is a sturdy pony,
A very mousy grey,
And all I can see of him now,
Is grey flashes when he is galloping around the field,
As fast as a racehorse at the start of a race.

He has a great little whinny,
And is always ready to play,
That's my Bertie,
The highlight of my day.

Karen Dooley (12)
Sale Grammar School